Reporters Under Fire

Westview Replica Editions

The concept of Westview Replica Editions is a response to the continuing crisis in academic and informational publishing. Library budgets for books have been severely curtailed. Ever larger portions of general library budgets are being diverted from the purchase of books and used for data banks, computers, micromedia, and other methods of information retrieval. Interlibrary loan structures further reduce the edition sizes required to satisfy the needs of the scholarly community. Economic pressures on the university presses and the few private scholarly publishing companies have severely limited the capacity of the industry to properly serve the academic and research communities. As a result, many manuscripts dealing with important subjects, often representing the highest level of scholarship, are no longer economically viable publishing projects--or, if accepted for publication, are typically subject to lead times ranging from one to three years.

Westview Replica Editions are our practical solution to the problem. We accept a manuscript in camera-ready form, typed according to our specifications, and move it immediately into the production process. As always, the selection criteria include the importance of the subject, the work's contribution to scholarship, and its insight, originality of thought, and excellence of exposition. The responsibility for editing and proofreading lies with the author or sponsoring institution. We prepare chapter headings and display pages, file for copyright, and obtain Library of Congress Cataloging in Publication Data. A detailed manual contains simple instructions for preparing the final typescript, and our editorial staff is always available to answer questions.

The end result is a book printed on acid-free paper and bound in sturdy library-quality soft covers. We manufacture these books ourselves using equipment that does not require a lengthy make-ready process and that allows us to publish first editions of 300 to 600 copies and to reprint even smaller quantities as needed. Thus, we can produce Replica Editions quickly and can keep even very specialized books in print as long as there is a demand for them.

About the Book and Editor

News media professionals, especially those covering political events or wars, are often accused of distorting the news or presenting biased and superficial analyses. Coverage of the recent conflicts in Central America and the Middle East has been especially controversial. In this volume, which is based on a series of seminars sponsored by the Institute for the Study of Diplomacy at Georgetown University, experienced journalists and media critics assess the complaints about coverage and the defenses the media marshall against those complaints. They explore the dilemmas that democratic societies face in trying to preserve traditional freedom of expression while pursuing political goals in ways that may involve the use of force. By analyzing the political impact of television coverage of battlefield scenes and the practical limitations and difficulties under which the media must work, the authors illuminate the powerful role of the media in the shaping of American politics, including diplomatic and military policies.

Landrum R. Bolling is president of the Inter-Faith Academy of Peace and was research professor of diplomacy at Georgetown University from 1981-1983. He is coauthor (with Craig Smith) of *Private Foreign Aid: U.S. Philanthropy in Relief and Development* (Westview, 1982).

Reporters Under Fire

U.S. Media Coverage of Conflicts in Lebanon and Central America

edited by Landrum R. Bolling

Westview Press / Boulder and London

A Westview Replica Edition

Copyright © 1985 by Westview Press, Inc.

Published in 1985 in the United States of America by Westview Press, Inc.,
5500 Central Avenue, Boulder, Colorado 80301; Frederick A. Praeger,
Publisher

Library of Congress Cataloging in Publication Data
Main entry under title:
Reporters under fire.
   (A Westview replica edition)
   1. Mass media--United States. 2. Lebanon--History--
1975-   . 3. Central America--History--1951-   .
I. Bolling, Landrum Rymer. II. Series.
P92.U5R46 1985   956.92'044   84-15267
ISBN 0-8133-7006-X

Printed and bound in the United States of America

10 9 8 7 6 5 4 3 2 1

Contents

Foreword

Television has brought war into the home. Particularly since the bloody fighting in Vietnam, the American public has been able to watch, in a manner previously unknown, the horrors and tragedy of armed conflict.

With this coverage has come debate, debate over the fairness of the coverage and over the impact of the coverage on our national will. Are we increasingly handicapped in the use of our own power because of the opposition to the deployment of force arising from a closer vision of the results? Or is the media an indispensable guardian of the public conscience and the public interest against irresponsible military ambition and power?

Two recent conflicts have heightened the debate: the Israeli actions in Lebanon and the American fighting in El Salvador and along the borders of Nicaragua. So, too, did the U.S. operation in Grenada, from which, initially, the Pentagon excluded the media.

Recognizing that the issue has a direct influence upon the conduct of our diplomacy, the Institute for the Study of Diplomacy at Georgetown University brought together a group of reporters and editors, plus scholars and critics, to discuss the coverage of these conflicts. What follows is a report of their deliberations, edited to provide coherence and to insure that all opinions expressed are fairly represented.

Selected excerpts from pertinent magazine and newspaper articles and occasional pamphlets that were distributed to participants are also included.

No conclusions were reached, but as the transcripts show, the significance and immediacy of the issue were clearly demonstrated. The transcripts and the attachments are presented here as a record of some stimulating discussions and as an encouragement to further exploration of this subject.

x

Our thanks go to the participants and to the many who helped us frame the issues and find relevant materials. We are especially grateful to the Gannett Foundation for its financial help for the luncheon meetings and this publication.

David D. Newsom
Director,
Institute for the
Study of Diplomacy

Introduction

Media coverage of the Third World is a topic that has produced an enormous amount of discussion in recent years -- often with considerable flashes of heat, sometimes with only flickering light. International conferences, university seminars, commissions of working journalists, and any number of magazine articles and monographs have dealt with various facets of the topic. A common starting point in most cases has been the proposed New World Information Order, put forth within the official circles of the United Nations Educational, Scientific and Cultural Organization (UNESCO).

When, at the Institute for the Study of Diplomacy, of the Georgetown University School of Foreign Service, it was decided to explore some of the issues related to media coverage of the Third World, we deliberately chose to set aside the controversial UNESCO proposal and to concentrate on a few of the operational problems and policy issues that are involved in the handling of certain major stories -- particularly Third World wars.

The arguments for and against the New World Information Order are clearly of great importance. They have been extensively addressed. The issues are of far-reaching significance to the less developed countries and to the media of the technically advanced countries, particularly to those with strong traditions of a free press. The fact that media representatives of the Western world and some information officers of the less developed countries find it difficult to agree on even what the issues are -- "censorship" or "controlled access" or "colonialist domination of the Third World media" or "Western trivialization and distortion," e.g. -- does not make the matter any less important or less urgent. It is part of the human predicament that we often find it more difficult to agree on what the questions are than to find possible answers.

In any case, we decided to forego the opportunity for another discussion of the explosive issue of the New World Information Order. Rather, what appealed to us at Georgetown was a series of seminars for working reporters and editors on the following topics: U.S. Media Coverage of Development Questions in the Developing World, U.S. Media Coverage of the 1982 War in Lebanon, U.S. Media Coverage of the Troubles in Central America, and the Impact of U.S. Media Coverage of the Third World on American Foreign Policy Toward Third World Countries.

Our first thought was to organize these meetings as day-and-a-half affairs at some quiet, rural retreat house. The Wye Plantation Conference Center of The Aspen Institute, on the Eastern Shore of Maryland, was made available to us for the first weekend in June 1982. As a meeting place it was all we could have hoped for. About thirty broadcasters, editors, foreign correspondents and other reporters experienced in covering the developing countries signed up to attend.

Our only problem was that we did not reckon with the disruptive effect of fast-breaking news events in the Third World. Specifically, we did not foresee the Israeli incursion into south Lebanon. One by one, our participants dropped out as emergency assignments called for them to catch planes or do desk duty that particular weekend. We thought we might have to cancel, but in the end we were able to bring together almost twenty participants, including a few people with primary backgrounds in diplomacy and government information services. It was a lively, at times contentious, exchange of views and experiences. Inevitably, we did not keep entirely away from the New World Information Order controversy. By the time we finished our second day's sessions, however, we had wrestled with a number of other serious media issues and problems. We were sure the effort had been worthwhile but were not certain we could do it again.

Thanks to the advice of those who attended that first seminar and those who wanted to come but could not, we did decide to continue, but to abandon the beautiful, isolated rural setting for a private club in Washington and to shorten the sessions to elongated working luncheons. We drank little and ate quickly, but the talk flowed swiftly and vigorously. Tape recordings gave us a record of all that was said.

This report is an attempt to summarize the various concerns, questions, opinions and recommendations that arose in the course of those seminars that dealt with coverage of the conflicts in Latin America and the Middle East. Although, necessarily, many of the statements have been condensed, all of the assorted viewpoints -- and they varied enormously -- are faithfully represented and the arguments accurately given.

In preparation for the sessions, "briefing kits" of copies of magazine and newspaper articles and occasional pamphlets were assembled and distributed. Selected excerpts from those materials are included here.

The whole enterprise could not have been carried through without the willing and at times enthusiastic and contentious interest of a number of hard-working members of the working press and broadcast services, academic specialists who are constantly studying the interrelationship of the media and the processes of U.S. foreign policy, and a few brave practitioners of the profession of diplomacy whose lives are, no doubt, made more challenging, and at times more difficult, by the attention they receive from the media. We, obviously, came to no conclusions, but we established to the satisfaction of all of us that the role of the media in the processes of making and implementing U.S. foreign policy is indeed highly important and controversial -- and deserves fuller, continuous attention.

Landrum R. Bolling

List of Seminar Participants

A group of correspondents and editors, most of whom had had experience writing from and about the Third World, including the Middle East and Latin America, took part in these seminars -- plus a few specialists from the academic and foreign service communities who share these interests. Those who participated in one or more of these seminars:

George L. Arms, Southern Education Communications
        Association
Robert Beecham, Chronicles of International
        Communication
Jeffrey Biggs, State Department
Ghassan Bishara, Al Fajr, Jerusalem
Wolf Blitzer, The Jerusalem Post
Bill Buzenberg, National Public Radio
Herschelle S. Challenor, UNESCO
Helena Cobban, Christian Science Monitor
Donald Critchfield, NBC News
Karen DeYoung, The Washington Post
Pat Ellis, The MacNeil/Lehrer Report
Mark Falcoff, American Enterprise Institute
Walter Friedenberg, Scripps-Howard Newspapers
Philip Geyelin, The Washington Post
Georgie Anne Geyer, Universal Press Syndicate
Frances Gomez, Foreign Press Centers, USIA
Grace Halsell, Writer
Jerry Hannifin, Time
Margaret Hayes, Senate Foreign Relations Committee
James Hoagland, The Washington Post
Daniel James, Writer/Foreign correspondent
Dr. Lawrence Kaggwa, Howard University Department of
        Journalism
Dr. Joseph Kennedy, AFRICARE
Levon Keshishian, Al Ahram, Cairo

Edward L. King, *Washington Times*
Donald Kirk, *USA Today*
Morton Kondracke, *The New Republic*
Charles Krauthammer, *The New Republic*
Robert Leiken, Center for Strategic and International
        Studies
William LeoGrande, Senate Democratic Policy Committee
Mary Leonard, *The Detroit News*
David Lichtenstein, Accuracy in Media Board
James Lobe, Inter-Press Service
John MacLean, *The Chicago Tribune*
James H. McCartney, Knight-Ridder Newspapers
Robert McCloskey, *The Washington Post*
Sergio Motta Melo, Brazilian Television
Carl Migdail, *U.S. News and World Report*
Bill Monroe, Meet the Press, NBC
Richard Nuccio, Woodrow Wilson Center
Ambassador Lawrence O'Keefe, British Foreign Service
Lawrence O'Rourke, *The St. Louis Post-Dispatch*
Rosemarie Phillips, Overseas Development Council
Wes Prudens, *Washington Times*
May Abdul Rahman, correspondent for Arab newspapers
William Ringle, Gannett Newspapers
Jeff Rosenberg, National Public Radio
Nick Thimmesch, American Enterprise Institute/
        Los Angeles Times Syndicate
Merle Thorpe, Jr., Foundation for Middle East Peace
Milton Viorst, Free-lance journalist
Ben J. Wattenberg, American Enterprise Institute
Allen Weinstein, Center for Strategic and International
        Studies

From Georgetown University:

Ambassador O. Rudolph Aggrey, Former U.S. Ambassador to
        Senegal and Romania
Ambassador David D. Newsom, Former Under Secretary of
        State, Director of the Institute for the Study
        of Diplomacy
Ambassador Martin F. Herz, Former U.S. Ambassador to
        Bulgaria, Director of Studies, ISD
Landrum R. Bolling, Research Professor of Diplomacy,
        Seminar Chairman

1
Questions on Media Coverage of Recent Wars

Landrum R. Bolling

In the early morning hours of October 25, 1983, U.S. combat forces landed on the shores of the small Caribbean island of Grenada. Whether called a "rescue mission," as Washington officials and representatives of the concerned neighboring island states preferred, or a "brutal invasion" as anti-American critics insisted, the overthrow of the callous and unpopular little Marxist dictatorship and the expulsion of the Cuban advisors, workers and soldiers was a major front-page story around the world. Yet this drastic and dramatic action, in its early stages, was not witnessed by any representative of the American media. Not one reporter, photographer or television crew was permitted to accompany any of the military units. A few intrepid reporters who tried by small boat to get to Grenada on their own were turned back.

The American public and the world had to depend upon official communiques and the random reports of a ham radio operator in Grenada talking to a ham radio operator in New Jersey. Within a few days, however, the American military authorities allowed small contingents of media people to fly into Grenada for one-day escorted visits, and eventually all press and broadcast restrictions were lifted as the U.S. withdrawal began.

Impassioned arguments over the Pentagon's handling of this information issue boiled up from the first day, thus setting in motion a prolonged and increasingly far-ranging national debate over the role of the media in the coverage of war actions. More accurately, that kind of debate had already begun over media coverage of the 1982 Israeli invasion of Lebanon and of the assorted troubles of Central America -- and of the United States involvements in those troubles. Indeed, Grenada revived memories of the bitterly divisive arguments over the American experience in Vietnam and the reporting of that painful period. It would be unrealistic to expect that such a debate will ever be settled to the full satisfaction of the media, the military authorities, the political leaders and the news-consuming general public. Perceptions differ as to what the issue is. The interests of the military and the interests of the media obviously are not identical and on occasion may be in direct conflict. The public sometimes favors one side of the argument, sometimes the other.

The military's case for severe restrictions on war coverage clearly draws upon experiences of the Vietnam war and certain other military actions since then. The basic argument is that the way in which a war is reported can undermine public support, sap the will of our soldiers to fight, and tarnish the national image. The failure to win in Southeast Asia, it is contended, was directly related to the broad, unrelenting and detailed coverage of that war by the U.S. mass media. Particularly the often-gory pictorial reportage by television, coming into millions of homes across the land, morning after morning and night after night, produced in time a popular revulsion.

The initial reactions of the American public to the Grenada media limitations seemed to support the thesis of the Pentagon. Newspapers from coast to coast reported that the letters from readers overwhelmingly expressed support for the initial ban on reporters. Editor and Publisher made an informal survey of about a dozen newspapers and reported a three-to-one margin in favor of the restrictions. Time Magazine said that its "225 letters on the issue ran eight to one against the press." NBC and ABC admitted that the phone calls and mail they received from television viewers indicated that 80 percent or more of those who took the trouble to comment on the issue expressed approval of the restrictions. However -- one indication of how changeable the public is, at least as revealed by the sampling of opinions -- three months after the Grenada episode began, a Harris poll reported that their scientific sampling showed that two of every three people polled -- 65 percent to 32 percent -- had come to believe that the media should have been allowed to accompany the U.S. forces into Grenada.

It is clear, of course, that so important an issue is not going to be settled on the basis of public opinion sampling. Certain fundamental questions about the way a democratic society functions, or should function, in relation to the media demand careful, deliberate attention in the interest of sound public policy:

Can a "free-press", democratic society defend itself and its friends and allies, in a dangerous world, against the totalitarian adversaries that do not have to contend with a free press and uncontrolled television?

● Are democracies to be denied the use of force to support national interests because of a media-fed squeamishness about the application of force in any and all circumstances?

● Is there no way to effect some kind of balance between the advantages a totalitarian government enjoys because of its ability to control or black out unfavorable news in warfare and the disadvantages for the free society of allowing open coverage of all the wartime events, even though it is almost inescapable that such broad coverage will undermine support for the war effort?

● Is it not essential for the carrying out of a nation's foreign and defense policies to limit the media's access to war actions, in the interest of protecting the lives of the fighting forces and of impeding the propaganda activities of the adversary?

● What rights do the media have to report directly on a war as it is getting under way? And what limits are appropriately fixed for its ongoing coverage?

● What right does the public have to know about and to "see" all the horrors of war as they are unfolding? Will the public not have a more balanced perspective on most war actions if there is some delay in the reporting?

Those are the kinds of questions raised in support of the military-imposed restrictions. But other questions are posed by those who denounce those restrictions:

● How, in a democratic society, can the public hold its political and military leaders accountable for their actions if there is not prompt and full reporting by independent media representatives who have access to nonofficial as well as official sources of information about military actions?

● In controlling the press, will not the military tend to protect the public relations image of those in authority and the political power of those who make the fateful decisions, sometimes to the disadvantage of the public interest?

● Is not the presence of independent reporters in war situations essential to provide corroborating credibility and assurances of honesty in the reporting by the military on the operations for which they are responsible?

● Ultimately, what judgment is a free society likely to make about war as an instrument of national policy, in a particular conflict situation or in general, if it gets honest, in-depth reporting of what actually happens in war, complete with pictures "in living color"? And does it not have the right to receive as much information as possible in the making of that judgment?

There are no clear and easy answers to these questions. They will be debated for a long time to come, and with good reason. Even within the White House staff there was lively argument over this issue from the first day of the Grenada operation. Les Janka, an assistant press spokesman, resigned in protest over the way the matter was handled, and others expressed privately their doubts and disagreements.

Where the media's coverage of major governmental and military affairs is at issue, opinions and feelings are likely to be strong on both sides. There is a built-in adversarial relationship between government agencies and the media, even in wartime, and that kind of relationship is bound to be exacerbated the more extensively the media delves into controversial policies and their implementation. The conflicts in Lebanon and Central America have been covered by the media extensively, in depth and over a long period of time. They will continue to demand major media attention for years to come, and that media attention is almost certain to involve continuing controversy. (Grenada, on the other hand, faded rather quickly from public concern.)

Nonetheless, the Grenada affair has triggered an extensive review of U.S. policies toward media coverage of military operations and provoked numerous public discussions of those policies. Editors, publishers and broadcasting executives filed formal protests with the Pentagon and the White House and called on the government to give assurances that reporters would be allowed to be present at future U.S. military operations. They contended that Grenada was "the first important military operation since the Revolutionary War that had been blacked out to the news media and, hence, to the American public." Press, radio and television gave the issue substantial attention.

In the New York Times of October 30, 1983, the columnist William Safire, onetime member of the Nixon White House staff and normally a staunch defender of Republican presidents and of the Pentagon, expressed sharp criticism of U.S. restrictions on media coverage of Grenada:

> Fearful of television pictures of casualties and impressed by Mrs. Thatcher's management of a supine British press during what I will now call the Malvinas war, the President dictated that coverage of his Grenada invasion would be handled exclusively by Pentagon press agents. He not only barred the traditional access, but in effect kidnapped and whisked away the American reporters on the scene.

The excuses given for this communications power grab were false. Caspar Weinberger, with an inarticulate martinet at his side, pretended that reporting was denied because of concern for journalists' safety, which is absurd: The Reagan administration would hail the obliteration of the press corps. Another reason advanced -- that the military was too busy to provide the press with tender, loving care -- is an insult calculated to enrage journalists.

The nastiest reason, bruited about within the Reagan bunker, is that even a small press pool would have blabbed and cost American lives. Not only is this below the belt, but beside the point: We know that the Cubans knew of the invasion plans at least a day in advance. In fact, the absence of U.S. war correspondents has curtailed criticism that the Pentagon miscalculated and sent in a dangerously small invasion force. The C.I.A. should have had a team with a radio on that island a week before the landing.

What has caused the Reagan men to invite a war with the press in the midst of two military campaigns? I should be writing today of the strategic importance of this timely invasion, which I favor and applaud; and here I am looking at my old friend Cap Weinberger with dismay. He is an intelligent human being, a good man, a patriot; and now he is...professing his abdication of control of the military on press coverage, which is a matter of public policy, and -- in my sorrowful opinion -- lying through tight lips about why he barred the press from the battlefield in Grenada.

David Brinkley, Senior Correspondent of ABC News, in testimony prepared for hearings before the House Subcommittee on Courts, Civil Liberties and the Administration of Justice, on November 2, 1983, stated:

Newsmen could have been taken in with the first wave with the understanding that they would not file until after the operation had commenced. This was frequently done in Vietnam and so far as I know there was never a compromise of a military operation traced to a journalist. ABC News and other news organizations have been ready, willing and able to charter planes and boats into the island, so that arguments that the military

could not support newsmen logistically are
simply specious.

In his NBC Nightly News commentary, John Chancellor, on
October 26, 1983, said:

> When there's a war on, journalism can be
> a risky business for journalists.
> But no journalism at all is risky for
> the country. The press, good or bad, and
> it's both, is a necessary part of the process
> of democracy.
> Every once in a while the press gets it
> in the neck, which is probably healthy. But
> the people who are happy that the press was
> kept off Grenada while the fighting went on
> ought to ask themselves: Do you know where
> your government is and what it is up to?
> Without the press, you can only put your
> faith in the official version.

A few media people expressed contrary views. One
of these was Pat Buchanan who, on November 2, wrote in
the Washington Times:

> The first imperative of the Marine-
> airborne assault was that it succeed, with a
> minimum of loss of American life. If
> maintaining the element of military surprise
> means keeping Sam Donaldson in the dark...so
> be it. Compared to the ultimate sacrifice
> [of military lives], of what importance the
> ruffled feathers of the peacocks in the White
> House press corps? When did the American
> press acquire the "right to know" in advance
> of U.S. military operation?

Three months after the fighting was over and
reporters had gained free access to the island, Jody
Powell presented on the PBS network a full and
thoughtful report on the whole episode and on the
public's reaction to it. Although the thrust of the
program was highly critical of the Pentagon's handling
of the matter, there were man-in-the-street comments
that indicated strong antagonism to the media and
support of the restrictions the Pentagon had applied.
One man, speaking of the initial suppression of any
news that Americans had mistakenly shelled a Grenada
hospital and killed several innocent civilians, said he
thought it was right to suppress such news because to
let it be published would "give America a bad name."

Earlier indications of this viewpoint were found in an extensive investigation of the subject by _Time_ magazine. In its issue of December 12, 1983, _Time_ devoted its cover story to the topic of "Journalism Under Fire," with considerable, but by no means exclusive, attention to the Grenada controversy. Its conclusion: "The dispute over Grenada seemed to uncork a pent-up public hostility. It reinforced a perception that journalists regard themselves as utterly detached from, and perhaps even hostile to, the Government of their country....Perhaps the most sensitive allegations of bias...that cropped up during the Grenada controversy: that journalists are not patriotic enough. 'You feel sometimes like they are not on your side in a war,' says John Lane, a former commissioner of Caffee County, Colo., who served in Viet Nam."

Although some military men have continued to insist that what was done to restrict media coverage in Grenada was correct, the Pentagon took seriously the criticism it received from the major news organizations and members of the Congress. It set up a special commission, headed by retired Maj. Gen. Winant Sidle, to study "press access to military operations." Questionnaires were sent to news representatives, seeking their views. A Pentagon spokesman, Michael Bruch, said: "We've got to come up with a system of protecting the mission but still permitting the media to cover an operation." The White House spokesman Larry Speakes gave a kind of left-handed apology to the press by making a public comment that "the media issue was overlooked in planning the invasion of Grenada" -- and that he had come to believe that "we probably could have preserved secrecy with a very small pool of reporters involved from the first."

In the long run, it seems likely that the Pentagon will return to, essentially, the policies and procedures it applied to the media in World War II and in the Korean and Vietnam wars. Such an arrangement -- with appropriate screening and accreditation, careful briefings, embargoes on the release of stories to fit the operational schedule of the military, and the use of small pools of reporters, on occasion, to represent the usually-too-large corps that would like to be present -- should work both for the military and the media. Grenada has been a problem, but that is not likely to be the kind of continuing problem we may go on arguing about with respect to media coverage of wars, revolutions and violence. The bigger, more long-lasting controversy over the media is best illustrated by the unending discussions over how reporters have dealt and are dealing with the troubles in the Middle East and in Central America.

MIDDLE EAST AND CENTRAL AMERICA COVERAGE
Clashes Over Ideology, Personal Loyalties --
And the Facts

Both Lebanon and Central America are clearly and intimately associated with vital American interests. Moreover, within the U.S. population there are substantial minorities that have strong emotional ties to those regions because of close ethnic identities with the peoples who live there. Additionally, many Americans see violence, revolutions and wars in the Middle East and Central America as Communist-inspired efforts to control those areas and to undermine American influence there and throughout the world. In that struggle the Soviets and their partisans are believed to have been gaining the upper hand -- particularly in such countries as Nicaragua and El Salvador, Syria and Lebanon. Moreover, there was, until the Grenada operation, chagrin and anger over the success of Communist Cuba in aiding the development of another Marxist government among the islands of the Caribbean.

American efforts to check hostile trends in all these regions have required the investment of considerable money, political capital and even some American lives. Yet success has continued to elude us -- until Grenada, if we now generally call that a success. Our most painful and expensive experience of failure, of course, came in Vietnam. The resulting feelings of frustration and anger have been powerful, pervasive and debilitating for the body politic.

What is wrong? Why cannot a nation of such vast wealth, power and good intentions accomplish its purposes more promptly and more effectively? Why cannot the United States assure victory for its friends and defeat for its enemies -- and the quick restoration of stability and order? (This is precisely what the Reagan administration attempted to do in Grenada -- and carried out, it believes, successfully. Some of the military argue that the relative success, promptly accomplished there, was in part attributable to the limitations imposed upon the media in covering Grenada.) So -- why haven't we been more successful in the carrying out of our foreign policies in support of freedom and in opposition to Marxist revolutions and Soviet expansionism?

Many answers are offered. The most popular seems to be some variant of the accusation that the United States has lost its conviction, its sense of commitment, its national purpose and its national will. Particular political leaders, or parties, or presidential administrations or majorities in the Congress are singled out for blame because of statements, executive actions or legislative enactments that are said to have encouraged our adversaries and frustrated efforts to protect the national interest. Thus, through our own behavior, we repeatedly undercut what are presumed to be our crucial foreign policy objectives. So the argument goes. Over the past three decades numerous charges have been voiced about who "lost Eastern Europe," who "lost China," who "lost" any number of other countries including Cuba, Angola, Ethiopia, Iran -- and, of course, Laos, Cambodia and Vietnam, and, for a time, little Grenada. We have been assailed by fears that we are about to "lose" Central America and the Middle East. Again, we are gripped by powerful feelings as we debate the issues.

Both those who most persistently raise the questions and those who object to the way they are raised generally agree that the American political processes are complicated and that influence and power are widely dispersed. It is clear that numerous and diverse individuals and institutions are usually involved in the making of whatever comes to be the national position on any international issue. And all of this means that every participant in the process can, with considerable justification, disclaim ultimate responsibility; for, indeed, under our decentralized system of governmental checks and balances, no official or group of officials is seen as having final authority.

Moreover, as servants of a democratic society, American political leaders, particularly those in the Congress, often can, and do, assert that they are simply responding to the wishes of concerned constituencies when they act a certain way on foreign aid, arms supplies or any number of other international issues. But how do those various popular constituencies determine their views on foreign policy questions? And how, for that matter, do the members of the Congress determine their private judgments on these matters? Here, again, there is broad agreement: the information and opinion provided by the media have a very significant impact upon the thinking of the general public and of governmental officials.

State Department officers have long had a rough rule of thumb for forecasting some of the issues they would have to deal with on a given day of hearings before Congressional committees. Whatever else they would be required to answer, they would certainly need to be ready to respond to questions prompted by relevant stories in that morning's (or some other recent) edition of the New York Times or the Washington Post.

However vast the official information resources available (and precisely because of their vastness), official Washington, like everybody else, gets a great deal of its foreign news, digested and analysed for it, from the newspapers it reads and the broadcasts it hears before or just after breakfast. Reporters and commentators who have readers and listeners in the Washington metropolitan area have an influence on national policy that is hard to exaggerate, although exceedingly difficult to measure.

Whatever else may be said about them, American media reports on international affairs cannot be counted on to echo the pronouncements of official spokesmen, our own or others. Such statements may, however, and often do, get priority treatment. Suggestions that they are ignored or down-played seem not often borne out by the facts. Moreover, some journalists in every era appear, at times, to become unofficial mouthpieces for the administration in power. Nonetheless, the official version of things has no monopoly in the public print where a free press prevails. On matters of controversy, contrary opinions are avidly sought and may, indeed, on occasion be given an attention they do not merit. The media thrives on the reporting of debate and more strenuous forms of conflict.

Yet the stakes are high in many of those conflicts, and how they are reported and how they are perceived by the public can have grave, long-term consequences. How does, and should, the media deal with its mission in covering international conflicts that are of life-and-death importance to the participants, that impinge on the vital interests of this country, that may affect the lives of many people over many years to come? What is its responsibility? What can and should a democratic government do to influence, control or prevent full coverage of military actions? These are sobering and not altogether welcome questions. These are the questions that have been asked again and again about the coverage of the troubles in Central America and in the Middle East, and more recently about Grenada.

Despite all the biases and special interest pleading that may on occasion lie behind the asking (and, similarly, behind both the accusatory and the defensive answers that are given), this issue calls for careful, comprehensive examination. The debate over this question, both inside and outside the media, is a healthy thing. Yet, clearly, there are more productive and less productive ways of conducting that debate.

Among the more dubious approaches is, surely, the resort to ad hominem arguments against the particular reporters. A classic case involves the late Herbert W. Matthews, veteran foreign correspondent of the New York Times, who has been accused of being the one American, more than any other, who "lost" Cuba to Fidel Castro and communism. It was he who tracked Castro into his mountain redoubt in the Sierra Maestra and wrote generally laudatory dispatches about the then-youthful and idealistic, humanitarian reformer who was gathering around him a brave band of rebels to overthrow the corrupt dictatorship of Fulgencio Batista. Matthews did not foresee and did not warn his readers that Castro was really a Marxist revolutionary and would in time fasten his own communist-style dictatorship upon Cuba. He certainly never predicted that Castro's Cuba would one day become one of the most trusted, most expensively supported satellites of the Soviet Union. He never hinted that, as an advocate of the spread of communism across the world, Castro would give aid to Marxist revolutionaries in such far-scattered places as Bolivia and Nicaragua, Angola and Ethiopia -- and that to the latter two countries he would send regular Cuban military forces as surrogate fighters for the Soviet Union. And, of course, he could not have anticipated that Castro would eventually play a major role (with Soviet and North Korean assistance) in creating a Marxist state on the tiny island of Grenada.

The story of Castro's Cuba is a particularly painful one to the people and government of the United States. How could these dreadful things happen to and through a warm-hearted people only 90 miles off the Florida coast? How could these, our friendly neighbors, be turned into such militant foes of the United States? How could they become a launching pad for revolutionary activities around the western hemisphere and a potential base for threatening the military security of this and other countries? And, given the vast disparity in population and power between the United States and Cuba, how and why was Castro able to get away with this outrageous behavior?

The assumption is that if the United States had had the will to act, Castro could have been overthrown long ago -- and his rise to power probably would have been prevented, in the first place. Why the lack of will? Lack of understanding of what was at stake. And why the lack of understanding? Inadequate, misleading and false information about Castro, his movement, his plans, his commitments. And where did that information come from? From our own free press. And, initially and in particular, from Herb Matthews of the renowned New York Times.

Those who make this analysis usually go on to say that Matthews was a soft-hearted liberal whose political perceptions were distorted by his experiences in the mid-1930s when he covered the Republican side in the Spanish Civil War.

There, associating with the anti-monarchists,

socialists and communists who valiantly but
unsuccessfully fought to block the conquest of Spain by
Generalissimo Francisco Franco, he developed a deep
sympathy for the left in revolutionary situations.
That sympathy, it is claimed, showed clearly in his
dispatches from Spain and, later, in his reporting from
Cuba and other parts of Latin America. If he had dug
more tenaciously and critically into the story of the
Cuban revolution, if he had probed more deeply into
Castro's beliefs and aims, he could have warned the
world of the danger of another nasty communist
dictatorship in the making -- on our very doorstep.
Such a warning, in place of the generally favorable
reviews for the Castro movement, could have made enough
difference to have changed our essentially passive
acceptance of Castro's rise to power. Had we known the
real story and acted promptly, we would have a vastly
different situation today. Such is the might-have-been
analysis by earlier critics of U.S. press coverage of
Latin America.

Echoes of that accusation of witting or unwitting
aid to revolutionary movements are clearly heard in
discussions of the coverage of the Salvadoran rebels
and the Sandinistas in Central America and of the PLO
in the Middle East. Again, it is said that sentimental
and naive media representatives have been slanting
their reports in favor of underdog revolutionaries.
Again, it is charged that some reporters are not
adequately informed about the complex political
realities of the peoples and governments they cover,
that they are taken in by the humanitarian rhetoric of
terrorists, that they fail to see that the injustices
of the regimes under attack may be as nothing compared
to the tyrannies the rebels will inflict if they win.

From a certain point of view, there may be some
validity to these complaints. Journalists are not well
prepared for predicting what will happen -- certainly
not in faraway places beset by confusing internal and
regional problems and afflicted with uncertain and
unpopular leaders. And even others who may be willing
to offer an opinion -- presidents, diplomats, members
of Congress, and the armchair critics of academia --
have few brilliant successes in international political
prophecy to point to concerning the Third World.

Moreover, most journalists stoutly resist the
notion that forecasting the future is an essential part
of their craft. That kind of thing, serious reporters
may say, they gladly leave to gossip and astrology
columnists. Part of the approved mythology of the
profession is that reporters simply write the facts:
their job is to tell what happened. If Somoza was
hated by the vast majority of the people in Nicaragua,
and a broad coalition of many kinds of people favored

his overthrow, those were the facts that had to be reported. If there were suspicions that the victorious Sandinistas would attempt to impose a Marxist dictatorship and make themselves allies of the Cubans and the Russians, that kind of speculation belonged in the editorials or in separate think pieces clearly labeled as "interpretation" or "news analysis."

The simple truth, of course, is that objective factual purity has not always and everywhere been the sole guiding principle of American journalism. For good or ill, newspaper readers have been, for generations, the captive audiences for some pretty opinionated editors. And not always have their opinions been confined to the editorial columns. The weekly newsmagazines, moreover, have tended to make no separation between editorializing and straight reporting. Through a careful blending of background research, colorful writing and skillful editing, present-day news magazines produce reports that are highly readable, carry a tone of final-word authenticity from "insider sources" -- and, often, pack an editorial opinion message that is highly convincing. Further, it should be noted that those newspapers that have foreign affairs specialists on their staffs, at home or abroad, have increasingly come to incorporate "news analysis" pieces into their news budgets. Even the wire services are turning out similar copy.

Clearly, editors, working reporters and the general public have come in recent years to believe that responsible media coverage does require far more than the mere recording of established facts. The whole investigative journalism trend -- good, bad and indifferent though its manifestations have been -- is itself indicative of a shift in both the professional and popular expectations for the media. Reporters have been given and have taken greater freedom in incorporating personal interpretive statements into their news dispatches. The results are, of course, not universally applauded. Reporters are damned for too much interpretation, and for not enough.

Still another criticism is that the men and women who have overseas assignments don't know enough to do adequate and responsible interpretive reporting -- and shouldn't try. They lack non-English language skills. They don't know enough about the local history, politics, economics and cultural traditions. They are truly innocents abroad.

Of all the viewpoints put forward, this was the one most vehemently rejected by a number of working-press participants in the Institute's seminars. It was emphatically denounced as a caricature that may once have been true in the World

War II period and immediately afterward, but, with rare
exceptions, is simply not true today. If the public
has not been getting the "real story" on El Salvador,
it is not because the reporters on the scene are merely
retooled Chicago police reporters who can't speak
Spanish and know nothing of Latin American history and
culture. Even snobbish academic specialists give high
marks to the intellectual qualifications of many of the
American reporters abroad today, including those who
cover Latin America.

A more seriously regarded criticism seems to be
the complaint that the space constrictions on the daily
newspapers and the time constraints on television
broadcasts make it exceedingly difficult to get beyond
the sensational, the violent, or the superficial in
foreign news reporting. The "news hole" is just not
big enough. Managing editors, publishers and
advertising managers are not prepared to cut back on
the column inches allocated to local news, household
hints and entertainment features, which are seen as
having higher priority interest for the bulk of
readers. The conventional wisdom is that except for
the readers of the <u>New York Times</u>, the <u>Washington Post</u>
and the <u>Christian Science Monitor</u>, most people have a
relatively low level of interest in foreign news -- and
very little interest in news from the Third World.
Whether that judgment is strictly correct or not, it is
clear that in most newspapers not enough space is made
available to provide adequate backgrounding for many of
the important stories that ought to be covered in
greater depth.

What is said about the print media is even more
pointedly directed at the broadcasters. Air time is
simply not available to give much analysis of complex
stories from the Third World -- with only a total of
twenty-two minutes available for all the news, domestic
and foreign, on the commercial news shows. Moreover,
the networks are locked in fierce competition for
viewers, and all are inclined to go for the dramatic,
often violent "visuals" that attract attention.
Concerning specifically the broadcasters' coverage of
the troubles in the Middle East and Central America, it
is clear that it is the "bang-bang" stories that have
the best chance of getting on most TV news programs.
Background, interpretation, analysis? Desirable? Yes,
everybody agrees. There just isn't time, within the
pattern followed in most of the television news
programs.

What seems to have most seriously concerned the
critics of the media coverage of events in the Middle
East and Central America has been the extensive
presentation of scenes of violence and war
destruction. Pictures of the wounded, the dead and the

dying, shown day after day, have produced public
revulsion -- directed primarily against those whose
guns created the casualties. Israeli officials and
their champions protested bitterly against this kind of
coverage of their invasion of Lebanon in the summer of
1982.

Without question, Israel suffered an unprecedented
public relations setback from those photographs,
culminating in worldwide criticism during their
spectacular bombardments of West Beirut. On behalf of
Israel, it was said that there was very little
attention given to the reasons for Israel's military
actions -- and no effort to compare the suffering
caused by Israeli fighters with the even greater
destruction and loss of life caused by the Arabs
fighting among themselves in the Lebanese civil war of
1975-76 and the Syrians' massacre of a reported 20,000
of their own people in the city of Hamma.

The response from journalists who have defended
the differences in the degree of coverage is that it is
all a matter of access. The Israelis and the PLO
granted access -- and, initially, the PLO more freely
than the Israelis. The Syrians did not, neither in the
Lebanese areas they controlled nor in their own
country. Similar arguments have been voiced concerning
the media performance in Central America where it has
been far easier to get pictures of the killings by the
army and irregular forces attached to the government of
El Salvador than those for which the rebels have been
responsible.

Overshadowing all these questions of detail about
the nature of the coverage of particular stories --
their fairness, their balance, their completeness -- is
another question that has emerged in numerous
statements by people on both sides of the argument.
That is: what is likely to be the long-term effect upon
the freedom of action of democratic countries, with
traditions of freedom of expression for the media, when
they are confronted by situations which, in the
judgment of their leaders, require military responses?
How great will be their disadvantage compared to actual
or potential enemies that allow no such freedom to
their media? At what point will democratic governments
begin to act more like authoritarian governments in
restricting or preventing immediate and comprehensive
coverage of wars? For the British that point was
reached when the Thatcher government decided on the
reconquest of the Falkland Islands -- and for the
United States with the Reagan government's invasion of
Grenada.

Obviously, the argument is not going to end soon.
However, there is a persistent and growing thought that
perhaps the world has come to some kind of public

opinion watershed on the use of violence to attain
political ends -- at least in democratic, free media
countries. When great masses of people are made
vividly aware of the hideous sufferings produced by
war, with an immediacy and a human poignancy that no
previous kind of reportage could approach, how will
they react? What kinds and how much of
government-sponsored violence will they accept and
support? What kinds of problems will their reactions
create for governments? What effect will their
feelings and their assessment of the issues, as shaped
by what they have seen on television, become a
significant factor in the making of war or the making
of peace -- and the long-term shaping of foreign
policy?

We don't know. We simply don't know.

2
The War in Lebanon

The incursion of Israeli forces into South Lebanon on June 6, 1982, the subsequent bombing of Palestinian camps in and around Beirut, the seventy-five day siege of the western half of that wounded city, and the eventual expulsion of Yasir Arafat's PLO fighters must surely be recorded as one of the most dramatic series of episodes in the recent history of the Middle East. As they unfolded, the media, local and international, covered these events with a close-up vividness and comprehensiveness hardly matched in the annals of warfare. The daily accounts of the war and its many horrors, presented by hundreds of reporters, commentators and camera crews, soon made it apparent that the media performance itself was turning into one of the biggest and most controversial stories of the war.

Passions were extremely high on both sides of the fighting. Onlookers, wherever they might be around the world, tended to become emotionally engaged partisans for or against the Israelis, for or against the Palestinians -- or just agonizers over battered, occupied and splintered Lebanon.

The Lebanese were at the outset divided over the Israeli action. Many of them, particularly the Christians but also some Muslims, welcomed the Israelis as liberators from the PLO. Other Lebanese were outraged at what they considered an unprovoked invasion, accompanied by massive destruction of property and wanton killing of innocent Lebanese and Palestinians. In time, as the siege dragged on and the casualties mounted, considerable numbers of Lebanese and Israelis, including soldiers of the IDF, began to turn from support of the Israeli invasion to anguished and even bitter criticism.

What had begun as a popular "defensive" war against a hated enemy, the PLO, became the subject of angry debate inside Israel, within the world Jewish community, and between the foreign supporters and

17

critics of Israel. The Begin government and its backers, at home and abroad, found themselves on the defensive as never before, with Israel under more open, sweeping and vigorous denunciation than at any other time since the modern state was established. Much of the criticism, they charged, was unfair, ill-informed, and based upon gross misperceptions of what was happening and why. Much of the blame for this unacceptable situation they placed upon the media -- both inside Israel and around the world.

Some editors and reporters, as well as certain outside professional observers of the media, associated themselves with these complaints against the performance of the broadcasters and the print journalists. Several studies, seminars, conferences (and countless arguments) ensued.

As part of the Institute for the Study of Diplomacy's project on "The Media and the Third World," it was decided that this thorny issue would be grasped firmly, but, we hoped, sensitively and objectively. We would arrange an informal, open-discussion seminar of "Media Coverage of the War in Lebanon -- 1982."

In approaching media people on the matter we received immediate and strong encouragement -- by those who had themselves participated in the coverage of Lebanon and those who had not, by those sympathetic to Israel's actions and those who were critical.

We tried, naturally, to recruit participants representative of diverse points of view. In large measure we succeeded. We fell short, however, on two points. We had very little representation of those Arabs and pro-Arabs who feel, and have long felt, that U.S. media coverage of the Middle East is, basically, blatantly pro-Israeli and that Arabs and their interests and viewpoints are consistently denigrated -- and who see no reason to change their opinions on the basis of the coverage of the war in Lebanon. On the other hand, some of the supporters of Israel felt that we had not secured a numerically strong enough contingent of pro-Israeli critics of the media. Though there was vigorous and repeated defense of Israel's policies and actions in our discussion, it was noticeable that the majority of those who participated tended to praise rather than complain of the media's performance.

The kit of background materials, excerpts of which are printed below, included reports prepared for the Anti-Defamation League of B'nai B'rith and the American-Arab Anti-Discrimination Committee, as well as a number of pieces from newspapers and magazines. Even as this publication goes to press, still more articles on the subject are appearing. Most of them seem to be delayed-reaction expressions of criticism against the media's alleged anti-Israel bias, and an American Jewish organization has filed a formal "fairness" complaint with the Federal Communications Commission against WNBC, New York and the National Broadcasting Company. Meanwhile, General Ariel Sharon has been staging a political come-back in Israel, charging that his personal political troubles and the failure of Israel to achieve its goals in Lebanon were due in large part to "stab-in-the-back" reporting by the Israeli and American press and television. Coverage of the war in Lebanon has become itself one of the longest of long-running international stories.

*   *   *

DAVID D. NEWSOM: The Middle East has always been an area where media coverage and assorted private views have been full of heat and emotion. That is no less true today than it always has been. We meet today after a number of events that have increased and intensified those feelings. In some respects, positions within that troubled area and about it have hardened. We are not wanting to rehash a lot of old arguments about the Middle East today. What we would like is for our discussion to help throw some light on the subject of how this country relates to the rest of the world in terms of the process by which facts are obtained and facts are fed into the thinking of the American public.

People and nations all over the world are concerned about what Americans think. Now, the United States is not unique in this regard. Yet, perhaps more than any other country, our people are seen by those outside the United States as a nation of jurors before which other peoples bring their problems and their points of view, seeking the approbation and the support of the American public. That relates with special meaning to the coverage of the Middle East. Both Arabs and Israelis are greatly concerned about how their conflict is reported in the American media. The same sort of concern attaches to the coverage of almost any significant international issue. That's a fact one accepts.

But here are some questions we want to look at: What are the facts regarding the degree to which the media considers itself merely a collector of facts? To what extent does our media consider itself an institution seeking to make judgments on foreign affairs? To what extent does our media as an institution seek to have an influence on the way foreign policies are formed -- or does it even give thought to its influence? Is the media simply an independent, and possibly skeptical, observer of the actions it reports? Or is the media, either by its own purposes or by default, a co-opted actor in American diplomacy and policy making? Those are some of the background questions we may want to keep in mind for our discussion today. I am sure it will be twisted and turned in various ways.

LANDRUM BOLLING: To state some of the issues involved here, we open with comments from two working journalists, who are also occasional critics of the media, and who have themselves written quite explicitly on the question of coverage of the Middle East this summer. First, Ben Wattenberg, a columnist for Universal Syndicate, also editor of <u>Public Opinion</u> magazine at The American Enterprise Institute (AEI), and a frequent commentator on television. He has recently discussed this question both on television and in his published writings. Then we will turn to Milton Viorst who has somewhat different points of view on this topic, about which he also has written.

BEN WATTENBERG: I begin the "twisting and turning" that David Newsom has suggested with a particularly tangential view of the prospects of our society for doing business on the international scene as a result of the coverage of the war in Lebanon. It was said by many people, particularly those you might regard as "pro-Israel" in this argument, that Israel was held to a double standard by the press in the course of this conflict. I must say that I agree, but the sense I have of it is that there is something more important going on there: that the double standard we are talking about we apply not only to Israel. It is also a double standard that we most unwittingly are applying exclusively to the free nations of the world because we can cover wars and the bloodshed that wars produce quite easily in a free society, but it is almost impossible to cover such bloodshed in an unfree society.

Now, war by its nature is an ugly, bloody, repugnant act. The war in Lebanon was, I believe, the first war in human history where the media, television in particular, could cover both sides of the battlefield. In other words, you could have a television crew taking a picture of an Israeli shell going off, you could have another television camera taking a picture of the shell landing in Beirut, you could have a third crew taking a picture of somebody crying or mourning, and you could have a fourth crew talking to Yasir Arafat who would have a nice little baby in his arms while he was talking to you. This is the only time that you have had that sort of an access. When you see bloodshed (which you could see in any war if it were televised) humane, civilized people watching it in their living rooms are going to be repelled. It is a very, very ugly and unfortunate human phenomenon. In a free society, exposure of the general public to that phenomenon is ultimately going to translate itself into public opinion and ultimately into politics and ultimately into policy. We saw all of that happen in the United States during this last summer.

What is most interesting to me, though, is not just that this was played out to the disadvantage of Israel during 1982 but that the standard we did apply to Israel we did not apply to Iran in the Iran-Iraq war -- because we couldn't get cameras in there. We did not apply that standard to the Soviet Union in Afghanistan -- because we couldn't get cameras in there. Dan Rather went in one day with a towel on his head and that was a wonderful piece of reporting, I thought. But that was a one-time thing. We could not get any sustained day-to-day coverage of the war in Afghanistan.

That same double standard we inflict upon ourselves, upon the United States of America. That's what we did in Vietnam. More recently, we surely, in my judgment, have done it in El Salvador.

Here is a very modest American participation -- fifty American advisors outnumbered twenty to one by the media. If you follow that war on American television, it seemed for a while as if it was a war about dead nuns, and then it seemed as if it was a war about four dead labor leaders. Then it seemed that it was a war about whether Alexander Haig was telling the truth as to whether there was -- my God, Heaven forfend -- really any Soviet involvement in Central America. Then we had a whole series of stories including an incredible episode where it was truly believed that a United States Marine was actually caught carrying a gun. Above and beyond all of that, of course, was the daily footage of bloodshed, bloodshed and more bloodshed, which is horrifying and which turned American public opinion, in terms of further Congressional aid and so on, against what I regarded as a relatively moderate and moral response on the part of the United States.

What this means is that if you believe in a free press, as I do, this is not going to stop; this is going to continue. The technology is getting better and better, there are more and more reporters out there, there are more and more cameras out there. What it means is that it is very difficult for the Western free nations to resort to force or to even threaten force because they know that it will be repugnant to their citizenry and have a negative political impact.

You could say that that is a great humanitarian advance; it lessens the likelihood of bloodshed, which is fine. But if exposure of the public to graphic presentations of the horrors of war is operating on only one side of the political divide, if it is only operating on free countries, and our adversaries know about it and we know that they know about it and they know that we know about it, they can still resort to force or, more typically, threaten to resort to force with few, if any, negative consequences for them. They know that we cannot credibly, or only with great difficulty, ever threaten the use of force because of the terrible negative reaction that will be stirred up in our own country.

In short, what this does, in a very serious way, is to change the balance of power in the world. Force is still one of the things that undergirds the nature of relationships between nations; how strong is he, how strong am I, what can I do, what can I get away with, what can't I get away with. When you say on one side of the divide that Team A has much less ability to resort to the threat of force than the other side does, then you have really tilted the balance of power in a way that is harmful to us.

Obviously, in our free society, not only ours but among our democratic allies, we gain a great deal from having a free press. I wouldn't exchange it for a country with a non-free press -- these are the bulwarks of our free society, and they make us strong in a hundred different ways. But it would just be silly, in my judgment, to say that our free press is a good that comes to these democratic societies without any negatives; it is a mixed picture. This sense of a diminishing of our ability to operate in the real world with the threat of force, the way nations typically have behaved, is something that is going to haunt us in years to come.

LANDRUM BOLLING: Thanks, Ben. Milton Viorst has covered the Middle East in various periods over the last twenty years extensively. He was out there this past summer. He has written and spoken about the media coverage of that latest Middle East war. In an article in the magazine Channels he has described his perception of the television coverage of the war in Lebanon. We hear from him next.

MILTON VIORST: I think it is very interesting that in the kit of press materials pulled together for us we have such a huge dossier of articles about -- not the war, but about the coverage of the war. That's unusual. We have generally not explored our coverage of events, the portrayal of wars in particular. In a sense, this is strange.

As to media performance in the war of the summer of 1982, it seems to me there was more controversial coverage, or lack of coverage, in the case of the British-Argentine War in the Falklands. If we are talking about dubious manipulation of the press for the purpose of achieving public policy and all those other kinds of things, it seems to me that we should really be ashamed of what Britain did as a free society in terms of what they did to us as an institution, the press, in the Falklands. It is interesting that there is much more debate on what is going on in the Middle East, and about the coverage of the Middle East, precisely because the Israelis have a reputation of not manipulating the press either as effectively or as deliberately as other nations. I think that is important to take into account, but let me move on to other points.

In all of these many articles, everybody, more or less, is attempting to evaluate the performance of the press. Now against what do we evaluate the performance of the press? When we evaluate the performance of the baseball player, it's not whether he hits a thousand in every game. If he can get up to some reasonably high level of human excellence, he's doing rather well.

In fact, the media, including television, in the Israeli invasion of Lebanon, did very well. They made certain mistakes -- some of them glaring -- yet, if we put this within the framework of reasonable human expectations for such a situation, I think we would have to say that the press can congratulate itself on its seriousness of purpose and high performance. It was unfortunate that it got sucked in, very early in the combat, into a game of number-playing: how many or who were rendered homeless, how many died in the course of the Israeli invasion. It was no doubt true that the Red Cross put out some figures which were not given proper scrutiny, and the press largely spewed them out again in the manner of our profession, the kind of thing we do badly. Nobody checked them.

In a sense, this is where the system most clearly fell down, and a reason it fell down is because this was the one period of the war when the Israelis would not let the press into the parts of Lebanon it controlled to find out what was really going on; so the press fell back upon all sorts of other sources which could not be readily checked. I am not suggesting that there should have been publication of erroneous figures without checking. Truly, the media should have made a greater effort to determine whether 10,000 really had been killed and 600,000 rendered homeless; these were figures that were being tossed around for a couple of weeks. But the interesting part about all this is that these figures were put out at the very time when reporters had the least access to the fighting zone. When the press did go into Israeli-controlled Lebanon, after about ten days, and were allowed direct coverage, then the reporting improved enormously. I think what happened is that, unhappy with the kinds of things that we said, like "War is not fun to watch on television," the Israeli government saw there was an opportunity to divert public attention with a squabble over the numbers. That one issue preoccupied too many people for too long. We in the media walked into a kind of trap of our own making. It should not have happened. Notwithstanding all that can be said on this point, I think television, as well as newspapers, did rather well over the course of the entire war.

To come to another criticism frequently made -- not a new criticism about television in America -- one of the inherent limitations of television coverage is that we are governed by a commercial system. The various networks go out and compete with one another for the best visual material they can get; as a consequence, they tend to come up with the most sensational stuff. But this was almost the same kind of problem we have always had with a free press from the beginning of this republic.

The argument for the First Amendment was the Jeffersonian argument that ultimately the truth will come out, even if there is a lot of irresponsible press activity. But in Lebanon, on the whole, we were not faced with irresponsible efforts to get out false or distorted news; we were faced with responsible efforts to get out news within a commercial framework. We have to recognize the limitations of television and to understand that what is presented to us on the screen every evening is really the most spectacular manifestation of a particular set of events that were taking place on that day.

Taking those facts into account, I am amazed at how accurate the reporting of the war was during that crucial eight or ten week period. I do not find any justification for the charge of willful distortion or bias.

I think it is important to address what Ben Wattenberg calls the double standard. I don't call it a double standard, though, for purposes of debate, let us accept the term. The fact is that the press does cover Israel differently from the way it covers Syria and the way it covers Uganda, and, for that matter, from the way it covers South Africa. Some people, in the course of last summer, insisted that this had to be a product of Western anti-Semitism and somehow, at the heart of all of this, was a particular desire to chastise the Jews. I don't dismiss the possibility that some reporters may have had such a bias, but there are other perspectives from which one can examine the problem.

One of the perspectives we ought to examine has to do with the definitions that we all here in this room give to news. I am sure we can at times vary a good deal on our definitions of what is news. Yet we all have a certain sense of what news is, and within all of our definitions there is this notion that news somehow has to contain the unexpected; if it isn't unexpected, then it wouldn't be news. If it is just some bureaucrat stamping a paper, then it won't be news. We have that element of the unexpected in our definition of news.

I think that what has happened in the coverage of Israel in Lebanon is a disposition on the part of much of the press to scrutinize and to criticize, often very harshly, the Israelis because they have conducted themselves in a manner which we have come to regard, rightly or wrongly, as unexpected -- out of character. As a relatively free society, over the course of many decades, it has received the benefits of being judged a free and highly humane society. It has justly been treated very well by the press. It is an open society where, for the most part, journalists can go anywhere. Moreover, the Israelis had a great deal to show of which they were proud and with which most of the Western world could relate. We are all, more or less, familiar with the origins of Israel and the value systems which it purports to realize.

On the other hand, I think that it is true that when the Syrians kill 20,000 of their own people in Hamma, there is a shrugging of the shoulders, a tendency to say, "Well, that's what you expect, right?" When the Ugandans kill a lot of one another, again a shrug of the shoulders. I am not defending this attitude. But I think there is a question of expectation at work here. Leaving aside the issue of whether they can get there to run the cameras or not, the media simply does not treat many of the horrible incidents of violence in some parts of the world with the same intensity with which it has treated Israeli behavior in the Lebanese War. I think it is difficult for us to face up to the fact of these attitudes behind the differences in coverage, but, at some level of our consciousness, that is the way we think and behave.

When the Israelis go in and initiate war and engage in the behavior which many of us found rather shocking, I think that we did treat Israel rather differently than we would have treated other societies for whom we had expected and accepted different standards of behavior. Perhaps we shouldn't do that, but we are a free society ourselves and we do make such judgments. I don't find it really very useful to concentrate on simply the factual errors of the press in relation to this last war. That is not the only perspective, or even the most important one, from which to make an evaluation of media performance. Much more significant is the factor of our unspoken expectation of how we thought Israel would conduct a war -- and what actually happened. It is within that framework that we must examine what the media reported.

LANDRUM BOLLING: Thank you, Milton. Before we turn to general discussion, I would just like to ask Jim Hoagland as an editor, sitting back here looking at the copy and making judgments about it as it flows in from overseas, to share a few of his thoughts with us.

JIM HOAGLAND: I'd like to pick up on a couple of points where I do have some differences. Ben, I wanted to raise a couple of details that I believe are important. One is that I think it is hardly unique that television was able to cover both sides of this particular conflict. From my own personal experience, I remember Cyprus, 1974. I remember Mike Nicolson of ITN driving out from the Greek side the morning of the Turkish invasion and actually interviewing Turkish paratroopers as they were landing and asking them what they were doing there and then driving back to the Greek side and waiting for the assault. I think there are a number of other conflicts that we could find that have provided roughly that same degree of accessibility, so I don't think that's the key factor at all.

You mentioned the press covering the Marine in El Salvador caught carrying a gun. I too was struck by that incident, but perhaps for different reasons. The reason that was a story, Ben, as you will recall, is that he was carrying the gun against the orders of his superiors. That fact -- that his superiors were ordering a Marine not to carry a gun -- says something important about the attitude of this administration toward the emplacement of those troops there, and their concern about U.S. public opinion. That was not a problem created by the press. We simply reported a situation that, I agree with you, was insane, denying a Marine the right to carry a weapon in a combat situation. But that's what this government is doing.

More important is your point on a double standard, and I also take a different viewpoint from the one Milton expresses. He suggests that we judge Iranian or Syrian actions by a different standard than the one by which we judge Israeli actions. I don't think that's true. We were following in the footsteps of the Israeli press which did an excellent job in covering what went on in Lebanon. We held Israel to no higher standard -- it would be impossible to hold Israel to any higher standard -- than the Israeli press did. It is not, consciously, a question of judging Israeli actions in a different way than we judge Iranian actions. I think Milton is right that there is a tendency to have different expectations about Israel. We may well express a little more cynicism about Syrians in Hama, but I guarantee you we would cover that story in the same detail if we had the access. That is the key, I think.

On the Falklands, I'm not sure I am as indignant as you are, Milt, about the British government actions. It was much more up to the press, in those briefings in London that did turn out to be quite misleading, to challenge the briefers. It is the responsibility of the press to judge its sources, to judge those statements, and to be much more cautious than we were in some instances. However, I do think we in America handled that fairly cautiously. Certainly much more so than did the British press. A government is out there to fight a war: they limit access, they censor the copy, and they make misleading statements. I would put the monkey more on the backs of the media; the media should dig harder. Perhaps we could hear from Bob McCloskey who dealt with it from both sides, spent years in the State Department watching the press being manipulated and now as ombudsman at the _Post_ is trying to defend us from that.

But the key question we face here is really the one David Newsom raised at the very beginning. The big issue is not to rehash what happened during the war in Lebanon. I suggest the really important question is one that most of us in the business have not given enough thought to: that is, the extent to which the media is vulnerable to penetration and manipulation by foreign actors for the purpose of influencing American foreign policy. I suspect we are vulnerable, but I would argue that what we do is far less decisive, has far less impact, than might appear at first.

If you take the Israeli invasion of Lebanon as a case, certainly the early stages of the invasion itself, we had a period of misleading statements from all sides. As far as Israeli intentions were concerned, there was great confusion about what was going to happen in those four, five, six days of the race to Beirut. I happened to be in Paris at the time for the Versailles Conference, and I can remember very well Al Haig's various statements that were based, he said later, on assurances from Israel. They were only going twenty-five miles, or maybe forty, or maybe sixty; each day it was a little more. I see no indication whatsoever that media coverage influenced

Israeli decisions on how far in they were going to go.
Even in the case of the siege of Beirut, there is very
little evidence, as opposed to speculation, about the
impact of press coverage on governmental decisions.

We do have stories of President Reagan being upset
by a photograph that was published, and the suggestion
was that this then influenced his attitude in his
meeting with Mr. Shamir. The result, supposedly, was
that he then posed for a photograph glowering at the
Israeli Foreign Minister. I think he understood it as a
public relations problem and responded to it in a
public relations way. The whole thing was handled in a
fairly superficial manner.

I see no evidence that this administration's real
actions toward Israel were greatly affected by media
coverage. I would say, indeed, that this
administration tends to care less about what the media
thinks about it than did the Carter administration,
which tended to react in a way that indicated they did
care much more. Perhaps that was a mistake for Mr.
Carter.

LANDRUM BOLLING: Before we open up for general
discussion: Ben Wattenberg, one minute, for a reply.

BEN WATTENBERG: Just a brief response to some of the
things that Jim brought up in terms of the double
standard. The fact is, five to ten times as many
people were killed in Lebanon -- not in Uganda, not in
Syria, but in that free country with free access for
television and the press -- in those years from 1975 to
1982, as were killed during the 1982 Israeli action in
Lebanon. Yet, there was maybe one one-hundredth of the
television coverage given to those horrible events as
was given to the 1982 Israeli war in Lebanon.

Secondly, what you say about the Israeli press is
absolutely correct and, in my judgment, bears out my
point. This is the nature of a free press, not just
the American press; it is the nature of a free press to
cover blood.

As to the idea that the Marine was not following
orders when he was carrying a rifle because it was
American policy that he should not be armed out of
concern for American public opinion -- that is exactly
my point. Because of the structural nature of a free
press and its role in a free society, you end up having
a government that is afraid to let a Marine carry a
gun. That is exactly the point: they were afraid of
that picture.

JIM HOAGLAND: They're afraid of the political
repercussions.

BEN WATTENBERG: That is exactly right. That is what I'm talking about.

JIM HOAGLAND: And that is the American system.

BEN WATTENBERG: Well, it is. But it is not a system that is without flaw or without problems. The Cyprus thing I will accept as an amendment to my comments. However, I would be very much interested to explore why the Israel-Lebanon thing got 100 times more television coverage than did the PLO-Lebanese-Syrian fighting in 1975-76 when that situation was open to television on both sides.

The last point is that the fact the press didn't change specific actions of this administration is not the point; it changed public opinion, public opinion changes politics, politics changes policy. That is a process. It's not something that happens immediately about which you can say: "Well, there was this picture on television and Ronald Reagan changed his mind." That's not the argument. The argument is that when you show what a free press is going to show: violence, which is spectacular, it gets through to people and they are repelled by it, and properly so. And that ultimately has a policy impact.

NICK THIMMESCH: I have a question for Ben and that is, when you describe the problem -- and there is merit in your arguments -- you take us up to the point of where we have to make a decision, where we have to take some action. What would you have the press do or say?

BEN WATTENBERG: I don't have a solution. I regard our meeting today as a consciousness raising session. Very seriously, the only solution is going to come from the people in the media. When they realize that the impact of their actions is enormous, and it's not just a ratings battle, when they see that we are really dealing with the fate of the free world, then, perhaps, we will find everybody taking a little more responsibility. However, I think it's a useful thing to discuss what the people who are carrying out those assignments and making those judgments understand about what is going on.

NICK THIMMESCH: Well, covering a war is not an easy business...

BEN WATTENBERG: I never said it was. On the failure of the media in Lebanon, as I see it, they didn't get the story wrong, they got the wrong story. I don't quibble with the idea that they made an understandable mistake on how many people were killed; that's very, very difficult, as has been pointed out. The question is why we didn't get this story put in the proper geopolitical context of what was going on in that area in the last seven years, in the last twenty years, in the last thirty years, in the last hundred years. In my judgment, the main fault was that all they were doing was covering the bang-bang part of it. And that was not the story. That is my point: not that they got the story wrong, but that they got the wrong story. There is a very big difference.

LANDRUM BOLLING: Next, Ghassan Bishara who represents the Palestinian newspaper in the West Bank, Al Fajr.

GHASSAN BISHARA: First of all, having followed American media coverage of the Israeli invasion of Lebanon, I would like very much to commend the American media as having done, I think, a very good job. I admire the press freedom which the Americans enjoy -- it's important for any healthy society to have a free press. I also think that is where the Israeli press has done a very good job, a tremendously good job. The Israeli press itself denounced their own government's handling of the Lebanon invasion. But even earlier, maybe a month or two earlier, the Israeli media covered the strike by the Druze on the Golan Heights where the Israeli press was not allowed during the time when the Golan was simply cut off from the outside world by the Israeli authorities. Nobody knew exactly what was happening there. And the Israeli press was very, very disturbed about it.
    However, coming back to the Lebanese invasion, I remember watching CBS News and for a long time I saw that all of the reports coming out of there carried the warning that they had been censored by the Israelis. It was important for everybody to know that Israeli censorship was a fact.
    There have been published comments to the effect that the Lebanon invasion was a real break in the pattern of Middle East coverage. Israel in its previous wars with Egypt, Syria and Jordan had managed the news very skillfully, while on the Arab side of the war, free access was not allowed. In this war, because what might happen on the Arab side was mainly under PLO control, the PLO very correctly allowed the media full freedom to operate. And because the PLO allowed free access, exactly when the Israelis did not, the world saw a different side of the story than the Israelis wanted known. The PLO saw what was good for their side. The PLO allowed free access to West Beirut when the Israelis surrounded and bombarded it, allowed the American and other Western media to see for themselves what the Israelis were doing to those people.

The other point that I think is important is that the results of what was reported in the media were not translated into policy. The fact is that in the U.S. budget decisions, in terms of what Congress votes in aid to Israel, there has been an increase of seventeen per cent in U.S. money voted for Israel just after all this media attention to what Israel did to Lebanon. So media coverage does not seem to influence U.S. policy.

WOLF BLITZER: On the question of the double standard: I think there is a double standard. And I think it has been demonstrated in the last few days through the coverage of the devastating earthquake in North Yemen. Why did the foreign editor of the Washington Post not assign a reporter to go to North Yemen to see what happened in that quake that took the lives of two thousand Yemeni? What would have been the reaction of the American press and the networks if that earthquake had happened in Western Europe? There is the double standard. The problem is that when people die, if they are Western people, white people, there is a greater sense of newsworthiness in the West than if blacks die or if Third World people die -- or, as in the last few days, if North Yemenis die. That is part of the double standard Ben Wattenberg was talking about. It was very visibly demonstrated this week; I was waiting to see if the major newspapers were going to send reporters to North Yemen to report on that great earthquake. They did not. They could get in. It's not a matter of access. It's a matter of people not caring. People don't care if North Yemenis die. People would care if they were dying in Western Europe or in the United States.

JIM HOAGLAND: I think that is a very callous judgment: people don't care if Yemenis die. I don't agree.

WOLF BLITZER: Then why didn't the Washington Post send somebody to North Yemen?

JIM HOAGLAND: What you're talking about is news judgment, not judgments about people's lives. You're talking about the comparative worth of earthquakes, if I understand you correctly, to the readership. You make the determinations about whether or not the destruction of Paris by an earthquake is the same as the destruction of a town we are not sure has been destroyed at this point.

WOLF BLITZER: On the question of access -- I would agree you can't get to the front in the war between Iran and Iraq, you can't see the tortures and the massacres going on there. That is a problem of access,

32

but it is also a problem of expectations. It's not all that interesting to see Third Worlders, blacks or Arabs killing each other. And that is sort of a negative racism. I wouldn't necessarily disagree that we are putting Israel on a higher level; we are, which is fine because the Israelis do it and that's part of the tradition. But I think there is also a negative racism at work by which we tend to discount Third World people who are being killed.

MILTON VIORST: I think the issue, in spite of what Jim said, is not whether there is a double standard. The issue, as Norman Podhoretz has raised it and sensitized us to it, is this: Is there something sinister here, some singling out of the Jews, some singling out of Israel, for some harshness of criticism which would not have been applied to Burundi or Iran? And my answer is that that is just plain wrong.

CHARLES KRAUTHAMMER: I would like to say something else about the double standard issue. We don't have to go to Iran or Burundi, or some other exotic place, to find examples of double standard treatment. Also, you find cases in which the media has set itself up as the jury by which to judge certain events and persons. The term "double standard" can at times be a euphemism for outright injustice in dealing with certain stories, in covering a particular people. I can't remember a single serious effort to explain the background of the killings at Sabra and Shatila, any attempt to recount the history of the killings by the PLO and their allies of the Christian villagers they drove from their homes. Nor was it always made clear that it was Lebanese who were primarily responsible for what happened in those camps, not the Israelis, who, at worst, had a secondary responsibility. Why so much space given to the accusations against the Israeli military?

MORTON KONDRACKE: Charles's point is right. Maybe some representative of the networks could give us an explanation of why so much attention is given to the supposed responsibility of the Israelis for what happened in those camps. The ratio of space given to the Israeli role compared to the space given to the role of the Lebanese is a hundred or even two hundred to one.

JIM HOAGLAND: You can't back that up. That is an untrue statement.

MILTON VIORST: But I don't think that's the point. The point is that the Israelis raised this issue originally. Four hundred thousand people were out on the main square of Tel Aviv because it was something of huge importance to the Israelis and therefore its level of newsworthiness far exceeded the level of newsworthiness of reactions among the Lebanese. Basically we did what I suggested before -- we shrugged and said, "Huh, so what do you expect? The Lebanese have been killing each other for years." That is basically in the realm of expectation.

JIM HOAGLAND: If you look at the coverage during that first weeks, after Sabra and Shatila, the weeks before the board of inquiry, the focus of the coverage in the Washington Post was the massacre and who committed it. The first day, discussion of the Israeli role was almost non-existent. The second day's story there was much more focused on the question of the Israelis allowing the militia units through the line. During the week, we published a story with specific names of the leaders of the Christian milita units that committed the massacres. The coverage that you are talking about stems almost entirely from Israel's own board of inquiry. Those stories have included repeated references -- not extensive because there's not much to say, unfortunately -- to the fact that the Lebanese are not conducting such a thorough inquiry. One of our stories on Mr. Gemayel's visit to Washington included reporting on the fact that he did not make himself available to the press for questioning, probably because of his concern about such questions.

WALT FRIEDENBERG: I find it very hard to believe, but everyone else seems to believe that what we're dealing with are journalists who topple their leaders with large measures of ignorance or selective awareness. We're talking about the press corps individuals. We're not really well prepared to examine the historical perspectives, so I think maybe we should look into our own professional qualifications. I think they are improving, to be sure.

The first war I had a shot at was the GI Joe story. It was about something else. Those were the days when correspondents wore the tag of "official U.S. correspondents." I'll be damned if there was anybody who would work in Vietnam under that same label.

We have been in the Middle East. We know about Israel. We were there at the birth. The press has covered Israel from day one to the present. The Palestinians -- well, coverage has suffered until recently. But I remember a New York Times series about the Palestinians. And they found the typical Palestinian had two legs, hands, fingers, and aspirations. So that was good. What has happened to the press, I think, is that through a series of wars, and as our education and experience broadens, we have become less attached to the government version of politics anywhere. Today we are more concerned about reality. We are becoming more detached, and I think that's a good thing -- for our readers and for ourselves.

UNIDENTIFIED SPEAKER: When the '73 war broke out, we only sent correspondents to Israel. That was because of an attitude of the big city newspapers that when we cover the Middle East it's from the Israeli side. Now we've gotten very sophisticated. We've got correspondents in Israel, in Egypt and in Beirut. As a result of that we have been getting both sides of the story. That is what happened in Lebanon and I think a great many American supporters of Israel were upset with that.

MORTON KONDRACKE: I think that the same adversarial relationships which we are used to applying to our own government -- by which we rip our own society to shreds as best we can, believing it our professional duty -- we are now applying that to various countries around the world. And we're not covering the range of activities that we ought to. For example, the Bulgarian/KGB involvement in the shooting of the Pope is a story that has received very little attention in the American press. Other than NBC news, it has been underplayed everywhere. The story of "yellow rain" has been around a long time, but the press has tried to undermine the State Department and demand that the State Department refute it or prove it without even reporting the story.

I find it very interesting and probable that, as was said earlier, we do hold the Israelis to a higher standard. What came through on television was shocking, and the coverage was accurate -- but that's not the whole story. There was, finally, an ABC correspondent on the Ted Koppel show who reported that the Palestinians allowed coverage of the wounded and of Yasir Arafat, but never allowed coverage of the fighting of the PLO. But there was no indication on the news footage of censorship by the PLO as there was in the case of the Israelis. I recall no coverage until after the fact of what happened in Damour where the Palestinians virtually destroyed a Christian town. And I remember no coverage, or only late coverage, of the kind of government that the PLO administered over southern Lebanon. Television has done a terrible job of covering the history of the Middle East situation, of the 50,000 people who were killed in Lebanon before the Israelis invaded.

JIM HOAGLAND: Another inaccuracy in what Mr. Kondracke has said. He said no coverage of Damour. I assume you mean no television coverage of Damour.

MORTON KONDRACKE: I mean certainly no television coverage, and if the Washington Post covered it, I don't remember it, but I'll take your word for it if it did.

JIM HOAGLAND: Mr. Kondracke, it was a page one story.

LANDRUM BOLLING: I want to get back to the double standards question. I wonder if double standard isn't a misleading term in one sense. I wonder if we are not really dealing with a question of personal identity -- greater or lesser identity with one side or the other. This very human phenomenon could help explain why we show bias or a greater degree of interest in one particular story and less interest in another one.

This country has an enormous sense of identity with Israel. It has had for many years. We cover Israel so very extensively, in large part, because of that sense of identity Americans have with Israel. We tend to flagellate ourselves as Americans about various aspects of our own policies and actions we disapprove of. In part, we may also get involved in criticizing Israel because Israel is, in one sense, an extension of the United States in the minds of a great many people. This is part of the problem. We get caught up in the fate of Israel, in its interests. We cover it more extensively, probably, than any other small strip of foreign land on earth, and that has both its good side and its bad side. I wonder if this identity issue isn't part of the story. Any comments on that?

BILL MONROE: I think you're right. I'm amazed, astonished at this talk about a double standard. It suggests that we're deliberately applying some judgment to one country that we're not to another.

There is no possible way that Israel can be looked on by news editors as on a par with almost any other country in the world. Our identity with Israel is such that our viewers and our readers have an interest in Israel they don't have in any other country, with the possible exception of Britain, France, Germany, and maybe Canada. We have an extraordinary interest in Israel which goes back decades and has to do with a long-standing sense of identity with it, with a feeling of shared values, with our contributions to the Israelis, with an admiration for what they are doing there, and their pioneering spirit. We kind of see ourselves in Israel. On top of that, we feel concerned about Israeli policy and how it fits in with, or

clashes with, United States policy. We have a feeling
that Israel is in a place where we could get into a lot
of trouble. It is also a country that could lead us
into some new era of peace, depending on how Israeli
and U.S. statesmen work out joint policies. So, it's a
place in which our interests are such that there is no
way we can cover any event affecting only an Arab
country in the same manner we cover a similar event
involving Israel. I think we've got to quit thinking in
terms of covering Israel the same way we cover other
countries.

Ben Wattenberg was talking about a double standard
in a way that I think needs rephrasing. He was talking
about a double standard in relation to countries at
war, or in any region where a war is going on. You've
got one country that allows coverage and the other
country does not, and Ben was accusing the media of
having a "double standard" because they have cameras on
one side but do not have cameras in on both sides. In
a sense, the war is being covered lop-sidedly, but
that's not because of the application of any editor's
biased judgement.

BEN WATTENBERG: Well, I would accept the amendment that
there was not a "double standard," that there was
simply "lop-sided" coverage, but that is the whole
point I was trying to make. I did not say, by the way,
that there was a double standard only in coverage of
Israel. What I said is that there is a double standard
in the way we cover violence in other countries.
Israel was the case in point that was particularly
pertinent for the variety of reasons that have come up
around the table. That is part and parcel of what Mort
was saying when he referred to the fact that we had
torn our own society to shreds doing exactly this same
sort of thing in covering U.S. actions. This is a much
bigger problem than just Israel. It applies to all the
free nations when they engage in acts of violence. As
you know, we all have this great, crusading
post-Watergate spirit that, "by God, we're going to
shake all the rafters." And you can shake those
rafters and shake those rafters until you have one hell
of a problem. The press can shake the rafters so hard
that the whole damn building starts shaking. And that
is something that ought to be recognized.

Now, I just would like to make one other point, if
I might, about Jim Hoagland's interchange with Mort
Kondracke. Jim, you can, I'm sure, always quote column
inches about what ran in the Washington Post about
Damour, for example, but I would maintain, along with
Mort, in terms not neccessarily of the news columns of
the Washington Post but of the whole newspaper and
media system, that if you think Damour got as much

coverage as Sabra and Shatila, then you are living in...

JIM HOAGLAND: I made no such suggestion.

BEN WATTENBERG: Well, okay. So if you made no such suggestion, I just want to establish Mort's specific point that those things like Damour, that show the PLO's atrocities, did not get into the media loop as big items. Moreover, Jim, I must say that I'm astonished that the paper that gave us Watergate and the Pentagon Papers can say of the Lebanese, "Well, they didn't have an investigation and they didn't have a press conference; that's why the obvious Lebanese involvement in Sabra and Shatila didn't get much coverage -- but the accusation of Israeli involvement did." You guys have established yourselves as the aggressive newspaper along with several others who dig these things out. This was the biggest story in the world for a month, and you're telling me that the Lebanese simply didn't give a press conference about it?

JIM HOAGLAND: No. I'm telling you several things, one of which was that we did our own story identifying by name the people who committed the massacre, Ben. That is in the tradition of Watergate coverage.

LANDRUM BOLLING: Let us get back to an issue I am sure we all think is crucial here. That is: What impact does media coverage have upon public opinion, which in turn has an impact upon politics, which has an impact upon our national policies? With regard to this, do we see any significant shifts in public attitudes coming out of coverage of the war in Lebanon? Another way to put the question is this: As you get graphic, first-hand direct coverage of violence and you bring pictures of that violence into the living room every day, do not the resulting public attitudes do something to the freedom of action of governments in using instruments of violence as a means of accomplishing political objectives?

It seems to me that we've moved into a new era. It is true that wars have always been horrible. Bloodshed and gore have been a part of war forever. But there is a new phenomenon in that the mass of the civilian population now gets to see what war is really like. It gets to see what's going on in the midst of a bombardment. This is something new.

There has been an extensive sense of horror and revulsion in this country about this war in Lebanon. I think I know the moment of the greatest emotional impact from the media coverage. There was a CBS broadcast from West Beirut one morning in mid-July. I don't know how CBS knew to be there, but they were in a Beirut hospital in the middle of an air raid. It was a hospital for retarded children and geriatric patients. You saw the shaking of the building. You saw the horror on the faces of nurses and on these poor patients. You couldn't have gotten a more dramatic expression of what happens in war. Now, no one in his right mind would ever suggest that Israelis deliberately tried to bomb that hospital. This happens in war -- it happens in urban wars.

The big question that haunted me all that summer long was this: What happens to the pursuit of national policy by means of military force when those war events and their human impact can be so graphically portrayed to the world just as they're happening?

It seems to me this represents a kind of watershed. Now, we are not going to go back and give up TV coverage, if we can get cameras in. So again, the question: What kinds of political issues can a free society try to solve by means of violence now that the age of television is fully upon us?

NICK THIMMESCH: I would like to ask Ben what he thinks about this: Since the coverage of Lebanon has created a great negative feeling in the United States, how is it then that the Senate Appropriations Subcommittee has rewarded the Israelis by increasing aid to them by half a billion dollars?

BEN WATTENBERG: Well, Nick, as I said, I think you're seeing what Landrum was talking about. You're talking about a process, not an event. If you are seriously saying that political support for Israel in the United States and around the world was increased because of the nature of the media coverage during the summer and early fall, to use an earlier phrase, you're living on another planet.

Now, exactly how that will express itself in the political process -- whether Reagan will crack down harder on the Israelis or whether Congress will or will not do something -- I cannot tell you; I am not a seer. But to suggest that the balance of public opinion regarding Israel has not been altered is bizarre. The public opinion polls show that a shift did occur.

I was not at the hearings. I have no idea. I don't know what the full Congress is going to do, and I think it is entirely irrelevant. Do you seriously think that Israel's political position was bolstered in this country by the media coverage of that war?

NICK THIMMESCH: No.

WILLIAM RINGLE: I'd like to make a very short point. I think that in the 1970s you could find very few American reporters or editors who had ever been to the Palestinian refugee camps. You could find a number of reporters who accepted unquestioningly and ingenuously everything that Israel put out, or what they had been shown on government-sponsored tours of Israel. I think that situation, for one reason or another, has changed, and this is making Israel and its supporters in this country very uncomfortable. And in some instances, to be quite candid, I think it's changed the other way; now, some people are accepting everything unquestioningly that comes from Arafat. But I think if you had had a similar group to this one in 1970, very few of them would have ever been in a Palestinian refugee camp, would have spoken to Palestinian leaders, would have given the Palestinian cause any credance at all. We now see a change from that.

HELENA COBBAN: I just want to come back to what was being said about this new phenomenon, a watershed. It was said that people can actually see what happens in wars. What we're talking about is something very specific. We're talking about an American society which has not been the scene of a major war for more than a century. It's not in your folklore, what's passed down from grandmothers to mothers to children. Any European knows what happens in a war -- even my generation. I was born after the war, but I've been to Coventry, and I've heard my father and grandfather talking about what happened during air raids. It's part of our culture. You're talking about something specifically American, and when you come up against it, the fact that all these MX missiles that you're building actually kill people, and these things happen in hospitals -- I mean I find it somewhat naive that you say you suddenly discovered that this is what happens.

BILL MONROE: I don't think it's provable that the use of pictures of combat areas will prevent governments from using violence to solve political problems on occasion. It's certainly not going to make it easier for governments to do that. The Vietnam War came into this discussion earlier. I think the emphasis on this is greatly exaggerated. Focusing our talk on pictures and film wipes out memory of the remarkable reporting that came out of that Vietnam War. The names of half a dozen journalists are in the hall of fame of journalism, for better or for worse, because of the work they did in print during the war. My Lai had a hell of a lot of attention in this country, and there were no pictures.

Any press corps that covered My Lai the way we did, and went into it for month after month, has a right to cover what happened in Beirut, look on the Israelis as brothers, and yet have the same indignation about the failings of the Israelis that we've had about our own military.

UNIDENTIFIED SPEAKER: I want to say it seems to me that both of you are operating from the premise that the public might actually be upset by the exposure to the realities of war. I fear Ben's position is that the world should be made safe for democracies so that governments can operate in some kind of vacuum.

BEN WATTENBERG: No, what I was saying is that a violent world ought to be made safe for democracy. There's a very big difference. The world is violent -- I mean, alas, the world is violent.

MILTON VIORST: I'd like to come back to the Falkland Islands War and the comment that Europe has had so much experience with violence and we've had so little. I was stunned by what happened with the Falklands because we were told that England would have a more civilized reaction, not like the more vulgar societies would. But, boy, when Mrs. Thatcher's government had an opportunity to solve that thing -- and I think there were ample alternative opportunities -- there was a kind of war hysteria that overcame Britain that I simply couldn't understand and it worries me. There is some indication here of something going on, whatever the horrors of the pictures we see at suppertime, that shows people will continue to watch war notwithstanding.

NICK THIMMESCH: Mr. Bolling, may I make a point raised by my friend, Mr. Kondracke, that the American press somehow succeeded in ripping this country apart -- I'm not sure I understand what that means. Is it our coverage of the civil rights revolution in this country? Is is our coverage of poverty in America? Or our coverage of Watergate? Is this ripping our country apart? If the answer to these questions is "yes," I think that the American press is performing exactly the job that Jefferson envisioned for the American press. And continuing that, it seems to me that out of that kind of coverage has come a great reform in American society -- a great understanding and recognition of what's going on out there. If you want to analogize, look at the Middle East; you can see that we've now come through a long metamorphosis from one-sided coverage to two-sided coverage. We now have a very honest and legitimate debate of crucial issues in an enlightened manner. For that we can be thankful for the more aggressive and more intelligent press.

LANDRUM BOLLING: I'd like to make just one comment and then ask David Newsom to close the meeting. Among those who have travelled often to Israel, I suspect many of us have felt that Israel is way ahead of this country in directness and bluntness of media coverage of the problems and issues of the Middle East. As a long-time Middle East watcher, someone who's been going back and forth from one to four times a year for more than a decade, I just want to pay tribute to the fact the Israel has a spectacularly free press -- an aggressive press, in a society where the people are very independent and articulate. The debate about the issues related to Israel's involvement in Lebanon goes on constantly in Israel. I have not found a corresponding degree of openness and vigorous debate in this country about the Middle East and about Israel. As some said earlier, if one criticized the American press for its coverage of the war in Lebanon, what would such critics say about Israeli coverage? Israeli coverage was far more devastating in its criticism of what the government was doing in Lebanon than we got in the American press. That's a fact of life. And that, I suggest, is part of the price they pay to maintain a free society in which they can make the most candid searching examination of very difficult issues.

Finally, I come back to this question: How do we in an open, free society deal with great, difficult political questions, in the midst of a violent world, in such a way that we minimize the use of violence or that we restrain governments from using violence to solve problems that would probably be better solved in some other way? I think this is the real question. But one of the things that may come out of this much more comprehensive coverage of violence and war in the television age could be serious examination of the question cf how, in a violent age, a free society deals with the official use of instruments of violence responsibly. We don't want to undermine the chance to effect significant change, but at the same time we must be concerned about how to restrain governments from rushing in to use violence to solve every problem. Free societies cannot get away, I think, anymore, with the capricious use of violence to solve political problems. One of the lessons out of the experience of the war in Lebanon was that people were forced to ask again whether there perhaps was not a better way of dealing with some of those problems. And now, David Newsom, would you close the meeting, please?

DAVID NEWSOM: I told my colleague Ambassador Martin Herz that I have been diligently silent through this meeting, feeling that this was a time for those on the media side of the fence to do most of the speaking; for what they have to say is of great interest to all of us. We thank you very much for coming. I think a very important issue has been identified and discussed here from various angles and that is this issue of the degree with which modern coverage of dramatic and violent events has an effect upon the scope of our policy responses to these events. This is a real issue, and we looked at it from the other side. There's another issue that we didn't get into. I think if we are able still to find further funding for discussions of this kind, we may want to have a replay and look at the question of the degree to which the media is a target, by very active efforts, not only in the Middle East, but elsewhere, of manipulation to get a point of view across through the media. I agree, having thought a great deal about the subject from a policymaker's standpoint, that the actual impact of the media on policy is an indirect impact. It is an impact that comes through the creation of public opinion which, in this country, then acts primarily, but not exclusively, upon the Congress, which, in turn, acts upon the Executive. One of the instances mentioned today, the M16 rifle in the hands of a Marine in El Salvador, is an example of the way in which media coverage can limit, by its influence on attitudes in Congress, the freedom of maneuver of policymakers and of implementers of policy. I'm sure there are others.

Because of my years of service in the State Department, I've been highly conscious of the degree in which other countries and other movements are fighting their battles in and before the people of the United States. This is true of Middle Eastern and many other countries.

As someone who has dealt with African affairs, I would like to make one comment on what was said about the attitude toward violence and the coverage of violence being affected by attitudes toward race. I think that there is great attention in this country to violence involving black people in Southern Africa. This comes back to another point Bill Monroe made and that is that the degree to which the readers and television viewers identify themselves with a country and a situation has a great effect on both the coverage and the impact of that coverage. A very large American community identifies with the majority people in Southern Africa. That has an impact just as the strong identification with Israel has an impact in the way

Israel is viewed and the way it is covered. For those of us who have been observers here in this stimulating session, we thank you very much for coming.

3
Published Analyses of Media Coverage of the 1982 War in Lebanon

Beirut -- and the Press -- Under Siege
By Roger Morris

For many American journalists, and much of their viewing or reading public, it was perhaps the most searing and controversial story in a generation. Israel's invasion of Lebanon in early June seemed to begin as one more round in a familiar cycle of violence and reprisal, one more almost routine combat assignment in covering thirty-five years of war in the Middle East. Yet as the fighting wore on, the Israeli attack not only overran the PLO; as never before, it soon engulfed the media as well, leaving newspapers and television under siege in West Beirut, both literally and figuratively.

As correspondents spoke into cameras or filed dispatches against the backdrop of the smoking city, partisans of both sides -- and, increasingly, supporters of Israel -- attacked the coverage for omission, distortion, or worse. Networks and newspapers were bombarded by angry delegations. In the heat of conflict at home and abroad, journalists lashed out at officials and at one another; there was a visible end to innocence and illusion among experienced newsmen who had prided themselves on having shed both long ago; and truth often became a casualty in the domestic war over the front-line reporting. When it was over, there was a sense that nothing scarred by the conflict -- journalism, public trust, the Middle East, Israel's moral and political standing with Americans -- would ever be the same again.

For sheer intensity and breadth, the controversy fueled by coverage of the Israeli invasion seems to have few parallels in recent journalistic history. After relatively brief and meager criticism of the

Reprinted from the <u>Columbia Journalism Review</u>, November/December 1982 by permission of the author.

reporting as anti-Arab, the storm centered on what
Boston Globe editorial-page editor Martin Nolan called
"general angst about the media's coverage of Israel."
While criticism poured in on major papers such as the
Globe, The Philadelphia Inquirer, The New York Times,
and especially, The Washington Post, the
Anti-Defamation League of B'nai B'rith hired political
consultant David Garth to review ABC, CBS, and NBC
television news coverage of the entire conflict to
document expected inaccuracies. To the Jerusalem Post,
most American reporting on the invasion was simply
"political pornography." Even Variety was troubled, in
its own idiom, by the "serious short circuits...between
reps of the international media" and Israeli
authorities. Summoning Emile Zola and Colonel Dreyfus
to the fray, Norman Podhoretz, editor of Commentary,
eventually wrote his own "J'Accuse," an ardent defense
of Israel's cause in which he strongly implied that a
number of Israel's critics, notably New York Times
columnist Anthony Lewis, were anti-Semitic.

Meanwhile, reporters lodged criticisms of their
own. Writing in the Washington Journalism Review, for
example, Israeli free-lance writer Pnini Ramati and The
Washington Post's Jerusalem correspondent, Edward Cody,
deplored Israel's censorship and defended fellow
writers on the Arab side whose dispatches "tended
naturally to fill the vacuum left by Israeli silence."
But the profession's varying frustration and concern
with the coverage was turned inward as well. There was
"some merit" to the charge of anti-Israeli bias in
television reporting, NBC's Marvin Kalb was quoted as
telling the August convention of the American Bar
Association. On August 6 (in an incident discussed
further below), Thomas L. Friedman, The New York
Times's bureau chief in Beirut, cabled his Manhattan
editors in outrage when he awoke to discover that they
had summarily cut the word "indiscriminate" from his
lead on the previous day's Israeli bombing of Beirut.
The bombing had "the apparent aim of terrorizing its
[Beirut's] civilian population," said Friedman's
telex. His editors had been "afraid to tell our
readers," and the correspondent thought it "thoroughly
unprofessional."

Even after the PLO departed and the siege of
Beirut was lifted, questions about the quality of U.S.
reporting continued to hang over the scene. Unproven
by the critics, unanswered by the media, the charges
seemed symbolized by an article that appeared in the
August 2 New Republic, titled "Lebanon Eyewitness,"
written by the magazine's owner and editor, Martin
Peretz. "Much of what you have read in the newspapers
and newsmagazines about the war in Lebanon -- and even
more of what you have seen and heard on television,"

Peretz wrote, "is simply not true." Railing against "journalists [who] think themselves chosen people" and a "peculiarly American mixture of ignorance, cynicism, and brashness," Peretz's travelogue through the Israeli occupation of southern Lebanon and its official rationalization did not constitute an intellectually serious critique. His attacks on The Washington Post and on the major networks were haphazardly documented; his praise for the Times, The Wall Street Journal, and other broadcast news was largely unsubstantiated.

But were the charges true? Had journalists, in fact, misrepresented the causes -- and exaggerated the extent -- of the carnage that dominated the news from Lebanon? Had they, in the process of reporting the invasion, somehow betrayed an American ally, as well as their own standards?

...Long respected for its Middle East coverage, The Christian Science Monitor duly reported "Israel's awesome pounding" of Beirut, yet editorially the paper made plain that "Yasir Arafat is stalling." The Monitor also carried an insightful three-part series by Trudy Rubin, beginning August 6, which emphasized the neglected reality that the Lebanese not only "hate the PLO" but feared the Israelis would "start to act the same" and simply install "new armed outsiders to replace the PLO." Meanwhile, the Los Angeles Times's J. Michael Kennedy, Charles T. Powers, and Kempster filed graphic stories on both the siege and the "oppression" by the PLO in Lebanon, while, on the op-ed page, Kennedy wrote about how, with both the Israelis and the PLO locked in battle, a great city was "being destroyed by people who do not seem to care." Editorially, the Times observed during the early August bombardment: "Blame the PLO for the torment of West Beirut and blame Israel no less." (Letters printed on the same page accused the paper of both anti-Israeli and anti-Palestinian bias.)

In some cases, however, comparisons among the voluminous coverage only made more conspicuous certain unreported stories of the invasion. The Inquirer's Robert Rosenthal and Ellen Cantarow for The Village Voice, for instance, wrote penetrating articles on the West Bank and the connection between the invasion and the stormy Israeli occupation of that area. In a sense, the West Bank was the gallery to which both warring sides played in Lebanon, its politics explaining the passion of the two armies and its territory likely to be the next symbolic if not literal battleground. But this story went largely ignored, especially by television....

With the exception of early reporting by Hedrick Smith in the Times, coverage was similarly absent on another front of the war -- the U.S. Congress. The

silence of Capitol Hill politicians on both sides, not
to mention the impact of the invasion on close election
campaigns starting up as the fighting and the media
coverage grew most controversial, was striking. But
most home-front journalists tended to dive for cover on
the issue along with the politicians.

Not least, there was little reporting on the
fascinating "story of the story" in Lebanon -- the
burdens imposed by Israeli censorship, the conditions
under which the doubly beleaguered journalists worked
in Beirut, the sociology of their knowledge, the inner
politics and reaction at papers and networks as the
controversy exploded. It would have made vivid and
unique firsthand war correspondence in a war in which
the news media were a powerful force; but few in either
print or television even brushed it, the networks'
reporting on censorship being limited, by and large, to
explanations of missing visuals.

But perhaps the most significant unreported story
was how it all began. There were intriguing shards of
the story here and there. In the <u>New Statesman</u> of June
25, Amnon Kapeliuk from Jerusalem reported "hundreds"
of articles in the Israeli press presaging the invasion
and an interview with Sharon saying he had been
planning it since the previous August, while Claudia
Wright noted that U.S. arms deliveries to Israel for
the first quarter of 1982 were almost ten times the
amount during the same period in 1980, and almost half
again higher than those in 1981. <u>The Wall Street
Journal</u>, in an August 10 Gerald F. Sieb feature on the
propaganda efforts in the U.S. by both sides, noted
that Sharon had toured the U.S. earlier in the spring
with a booklet that, in effect, justified the
invasion. On August 1, NBC's Bob Kur showed previously
censored film brought out from Israel depicting Israeli
troops and equipment poised along the border in May,
well before the attempted assassination of Ambassador
Argov or any PLO rocket attacks of early June. The <u>Post</u>
ran fascinating excerpts of interviews with Begin and
Secretary of State Alexander Haig, just before the
latter's resignation, that suggested that Haig's views
on Lebanon might be closer to Begin's than to Ronald
Reagan's. Did the U.S. -- or at least some officials --
know about the invasion long in advance? What had been
U.S. policy, or was there more than one policy? Was an
American secretary of state one of the casualties of
the siege, and was he really a noncombatant?

Lebanon -- and the Vietnam Parallel

To Podhoretz and other critics, commentary on the
Israeli invasion of Lebanon revealed the same "loss of
nerve" that had afflicted the U.S. in Vietnam. Yet the

legacy of the Vietnam conflict helped to produce quite the opposite effect on journalists: a plain determination not to be taken in, to question official claims on all sides. Again, while Podhoretz argued that the press should have celebrated the victory of a U.S.-armed conventional force over Soviet-supported guerillas, the immediate Vietnam parallel for working journalists was the censorship in Jerusalem, which proved no more popular than slanted American press briefings in Saigon (where, ironically, one of the briefers was Philip Habib). Journalists appeared to resent in particular the transparent falsity of the original Israeli claim to be clearing out only a twenty-five mile buffer zone.

On the other hand, there was also evident trauma for American reporters, many of whom seemed, for the first time, to be seeing the Palestinians in human terms, in the blood and tears of the street and crowded hospital wards, and not simply as "terrorists" and "guerillas." As "the other side" took on human reality, reporters inevitably became sympathetic to the plight of civilians. Added to that was the shock of journalists like Chancellor and Farrell made evident by their allusions to Beirut in terms of Manhattan. For Americans watching a great urban center under attack, the first since World War II, the image was brutal and obviously close to home. This was no Asian village or Middle East desert fastness, but streets and apartment houses recalling lakefront Chicago or, as Farrell wrote, Gramercy Park. Moreover, the urban intensity gave what was television's war even more concentrated sights and sounds to compress into the medium's limited compass. In the smoldering streets of West Beirut, with its screaming sirens and people, television caught the story with rare fidelity. Altogether, the result was a story that showed genuine empathy for the suffering city, and dismay at the destruction wrought by the encircling army, however understandable its presence might have been.

But was that empathy somehow political? Would the press have been less sensitive to the story of human suffering if it had been the PLO, not the Israelis, shelling a hostage city? Would John Chancellor have been less inclined to ask "What in the world is going on?" There was nothing in the coverage to suggest a double standard. Although journalists vividly depicted the suffering of civilians, they continued to credit the Israeli justification for the invasion -- right up to the gates of Beirut. Indeed, they did so almost to the exclusion of that other history behind the invasion -- the Palestinian exodus and suffering since 1947. When the focus of the siege journalism turned perforce in late June to the calamity of West Beirut, the story

reflected sympathy not for the entrenched PLO but for
the innocent people among whose demolished homes the
two sides fought.

When the invasion and the siege story were over,
much seemed buried in West Beirut -- the old PLO,
perhaps the old Israel, perhaps the innocence of the
media, something almost certainly too of American
foreign policy -- but it was a graveyard as well of the
critics' charges of unprofessional reporting. In June,
American journalism came to a bloody new war in the
Middle East, reported what it saw for the most part
fairly and accurately and sometimes brilliantly,
provided balanced comment, and provoked and absorbed
controversy. For performance under fire, readers and
viewers could have asked for little more.

Covering the Invasion of Lebanon:
Israel's Credibility is a Casualty of the First
Mid-East War Reported from Both Sides
By Edward Cody and Pnina Ramati

When Israeli tanks rolled north into Lebanon, a
correspondent watching them stream across the border
remarked, "Well, the story has just rumbled over to the
other side."

The troubles began on that first day.
Correspondents who sought to relay news of the armored
wave sweeping across southern Lebanon found their
telephone lines cut by Israeli censors monitoring
calls. By the time they returned to Jerusalem or Tel
Aviv to skirt the monitoring, the Israeli government
had made a skeletal announcement of its attack. But
also by then, correspondents in Beirut were filing away
with vivid, on-the-spot reports. It was the first
instance of what was to become a pattern....

For the first time in a major Arab-Israeli
conflict, reporters on the Arab side had relatively
free access to at least part of the battlefront.
Moreover, they dispatched their stories free of
censorship....

The situation on Israeli-Palestinian fronts
differed from those where Syria was involved.
Reporters could not follow the high-altitude aerial
encounters that led to defeat of the Syrian air force.
They were unable to see much of the tank battles in the
Bekaa Valley. Coupled with silence in Damascus, this
left the field free for Israel's version of what went
on....

But along the coast where the Palestinian Libera-

Reprinted from the Washington Journalism Review,
September 1982.

tion Organization was involved, reporters could witness much of the action for themselves...and Palestinian guerrillas were mixed with Lebanese civilians so tightly that ugly casualties were inevitable. The close access and dramatic content increased the relative newsworthiness of reports from Lebanon. This was particularly true when they came in alongside reports from the Israeli side, at first confined to army statements,...that casualties were as high as reported from Beirut....

Israeli censors... began cutting out footage of damage to civilian areas wrought by Israeli planes and cannons. On one occasion, they refused outright to allow transmission of an interview with PLO leader Yassir Arafat -- part of which was later broadcast on Israeli government television. After American networks began showing blanked-out space to dramatize what censors had cut, the Israeli government refused to transmit any Beirut footage at all....

Israeli officials' frequent charges of press hostility were aimed primarily at television....

Besides the medium, there was something different about the message in this conflict. The television footage was showing Israeli warplanes and artillery in repeated bombardment of civilian-populated areas, particularly Beirut. Israeli officials expressed dismay that, in their view, correspondents and television film focused on consequences of the battle rather than the battle itself....The point of the invasion...was to destroy an enemy. But most reports from Beirut and most correspondents in Israel concentrated on the means -- bombardments that took civilian casualties and destroyed civilian homes. This was not the image of themselves that the Israelis had grown used to, and not the image that they were used to displaying in Europe and the United States....

An Anti-Defamation League of B'nai B'rith Study
October 1982
"Television Network Coverage of the War in Lebanon"

Our study raised some questions which we believe may be of interest:

1) The American media are no longer mere spectators -- they have become a factor in shaping public opinion, and, in some cases, U.S. foreign policy. In light of these developments, do the media need to formulate a new set of responsibilities toward the viewing public, or are they on the right track already?

Reprinted by permission of the Anti-Defamation League of B'nai B'rith.

2) As television devotes more and more time to news reporting, is the quality of news reporting constantly improving? How much more of a factor is news reporting in determining public opinion and governmental policy?

3) Should the networks have reported the war in any particular context? Is straight, objective reporting possible in a hot war? Elements such as tone of voice, choice of adjectives and editing ultimately play a role in creating a final impression -- intended or not.

4) Since Israel is a democracy and the Arab states are not, it has become commonplace for the media to judge Israel by different standards than those used to judge the Arab world. While the thinking behind this may be understandable, it raises a basic and fundamental question: In using one set of standards for Israel and a different set for the Palestine Liberation Organization and Arab countries, how can the viewer accurately judge the right and wrong of the situation?

5) To what extent, if any, were the media manipulated and/or intimidated by the P.L.O. and Yasir Arafat during the seven-year Lebanese civil war, and during the recent war in Lebanon? What kind of censorship was imposed by the P.L.O., implicit or explicit?

6) How much were internal Israeli decisions regarding military censorship, public relations, and the conduct of the war responsible for the way the war was reported by the American media?...

The examination of network news coverage is divided into three categories:

1. Accuracy of Reporting
2. Censorship
3. Balance and Fairness

1) Accuracy of Reporting

The greatest inaccuracies in reporting related to casualty figures. This was found to be a major problem in network news coverage in June. In July and August, improvement was noted. During June (specifically during the ten days after the outbreak of war, when Israel did not release any casualty figures), there were many occasions when ABC, NBC, and CBS reports cited casualty figures without providing a source....For example, while the networks initially reported that there were 600,000 refugees in Southern Lebanon, the International Committee of the Red Cross stated on June 18 that this figure was highly exaggerated and gave its conclusion that 300,000 were made homeless. No network reported this update....On innumerable occasions in the June coverage of the war, reporters in the field and anchormen used the Palestinian Red Crescent interchangeably with the Red Cross. Exception must be taken for two specific reasons: First, the Red Crescent in Lebanon is not an independent humanitarian organization: rather, it is an arm of the Palestine Liberation Organization. Second, the head of the Red Crescent is Fathi Arafat, the brother of the P.L.O. chairman Yasir Arafat....

2) Censorship

Israeli censorship was a factor in network reporting, but it appears to have been overplayed. ADL believes that the way the three networks treated the censorship issue went beyond normal journalistic practice. On many occasions, superimposing "Report cleared by Israeli censors" on field reports, the anchormen of each network indicated before airing the story that the upcoming report had been censored; this was often followed by the field reporter again reminding the viewer that the report was censored. In addition, on a number of occasions after Israel banned ABC transmissions, NBC and CBS showed blacked-out screens with the words "PICTURES CENSORED" in bold type or "22 seconds deleted by Israeli censors." It seemed that the networks were trying to retaliate against what they thought were arbitrary Israeli practices. We believe that was also beyond normal journalistic practices.

At the time the networks were reporting the Lebanese conflict, they were also covering a war in which another democratic country was engaged -- Britain in the Falklands. An examination and comparison of the way the networks treated censorship in the Falklands with their treatment of Israeli censorship would indicate that, indeed, very different standards were employed. (This is just an impression. It is not the result of an in-depth study.)

While the networks, and all journalists, informed their viewers and readers that their war reports were subject to Israeli censorship, there was another type of censorship which was not reported. During the period when the P.L.O. controlled West Beirut, the freedom of correspondents was limited by what the P.L.O. wanted them to report and film. They were not permitted to film various arms caches and other P.L.O. strongholds if the P.L.O. did not choose to take them there. In short, while there was no P.L.O. censor sitting next to the correspondent during the transmission of the report (as was the case in Israel), there was a widespread degree of network self-censorship, since reporters were not free to roam the streets of Beirut and shoot film at will, and that fact was not often or as dramatically reported as was Israeli censorship.

3) Balance and Fairness

The question of balance and fairness is the most difficult issue to analyze. One person's fairness is another's distortion. While the issue is extremely difficult to place in perspective, we believe that all of the networks, perhaps unwittingly or unconsciously, contributed to some distortion and lack of objective perspective in their coverage of the war. A number of basic observations highlight our concern.

a) Network news, seeking visually powerful images, instinctively pursues the hot or graphic story, wherever it occurs.

The "hot news" stories always assumed priority in the nightly news broadcasts. They were not balanced with enough stories of events in Southern Lebanon, or even with the strategically more important story of the Syrian-Israeli battle in the Bekaa Valley. Surely the tank battles and dogfights between Israel and Syria were of long-range importance and interest to the United States and the West. Yet, these stories were not adequately covered because the networks were unable to get cameras in and, therefore, there were either no visuals or visuals not as intense as those in Beirut.

b) Since many important world events are not accessible to American cameras, the Lebanese war, an international event in which the networks could cover both sides, became the centerpiece for the evening news. Because cameras were barred in Afghanistan, Somalia, Iran or Iraq, the networks were not able to cover these wars revealingly and consequently could not focus on their importance to the American viewer with the force and clarity that they devoted to the Lebanon conflict....

c) Rarely was it mentioned that the P.L.O. intentionally placed its artillery within civilian centers, or that the Israelis had taken extraordinary measures to avoid civilian casualties, such as warning civilians before an attack to flee to the beaches for safety. In addition, Israeli relief efforts (an extraordinary departure from the usual behavior of combatants and certainly newsworthy) were not adequately reported....

d) The war was not placed in sufficient historical perspective. Generally speaking, the networks did not report the conflict in Lebanon in the context of the larger political and historical realities of the region. For example, CBS began its report about the war on June 4 by referring to Israel's July, 1981 bombing of Beirut in which 300 civilians were reported to have been killed. The networks generally did not report this conflict in the context of the seven-year civil war in which 100,000 Christians and Palestinians were killed, or of Jordan's expulsion of the Palestinians in 1970 in which 10,000 Palestinians were reportedly killed....

e) Many network reporters focused on -- and exaggerated -- internal Israeli debate over the war. Although there was a major pro-government rally in Israel at the beginning of July which was reported, anchormen and reporters continued to emphasize divisions in Israeli public opinion regarding the war. Thus, NBC correspondent John Hart reported on July 3 that "...this question of attacking West Beirut had divided the Israeli people almost down the middle."

Although it was unprecedented for Israelis to protest a war while the troops were not yet home, and the networks had an obligation to report this, not enough attention was devoted to the fact that the overwhelming majority of Israelis solidly supported the Begin government. Also, this was the first war in Israeli history under a Likud administration. Since a majority of the war protestors were opponents of the Likud government, so indicating would have placed the issue in a more revealing context.

Overview

Television reporting of the Lebanese war in June can be questioned on two counts: 1) not putting the war into perspective; 2) reporting inflated casualty figures. Network reports in July on the Lebanese war reflected a shift in emphasis and, to a subtle degree, in style as the fighting became sporadic, the siege continued, and the negotiations dragged on.

By July, casualty figures were not being reported often. When they were, sources were generally cited. Whereas in June the issue of censorship was dramatized, by July this was no longer the case. Moreover, the networks were careful to indicate that some reports had been cleared by Syrian censors. The balance issue, however, continued to dominate the July and August network coverage.

During these months, after viewing all of the reports on the Lebanese war, the main sentiment which emerged from the coverage was one of revulsion at the violence which was implicitly or explicitly associated with Israel. Even if the text of a report correctly attributed the violence to the P.L.O. or leftist Moslem militias, the brutally graphic visuals of explosions, suffering refugees, women, children, and the wounded, tended to obscure and overwhelm the text. Scenes of violence were inevitably and reflexively linked to Israel, however inadvertently and however understandably in a situation where the media competes for "scoops" and graphic depiction of violent events. There was perhaps too often a willingness to show violence without any counterbalancing explanation....

During July, there were interviews with P.L.O. spokesmen. Given Arafat's intentionally high visibility during this period, one can understand why he was interviewed and photographed so frequently. However, many of these reports tended to portray the P.L.O. in a romanticized light, as determined resisters ("freedom fighters") and Arafat as a typical, savvy "politician," trying to please his constituents. This was visually reinforced with repeated shots of Arafat kissing babies, smiling broadly, etc. Although Arafat's rhetoric in these apparently spontaneous interviews was standard and calculated for effect, it was aired repeatedly, with little or no analysis of its propaganda aspect.

In summary, all of the following factors contributed to our perception of a lack of balance in the news media's handling of Israel's actions in Lebanon:

● inflated casualty figures reported and not corrected, as well as other factual errors;

● melodramatic portrayal of Israeli censorship;

● lingering and graphic daily coverage of the wounded and suffering that overwhelmed or overlooked the political, historical and military context of the situation;

● simple, nondimensional reporting of P.L.O. posturing and a lack of critical analysis of the nature and the background of the P.L.O. role.

American-Arab Anti-Discrimination Committee
ADC Issue No.10
"U.S. Press Coverage of the Israeli
Invasion of Lebanon"
By Eric Hooglund

A review of the coverage by major U.S. daily newspapers of the Israeli invasion of Lebanon reveals a consistent pro-Israeli bias. This bias is evidenced in several ways. The most important, but also the most subtle, manner in which the press demonstrates its favor for Israel is through the daily editorial decision making process,...the choice of words for headlines and other captions, the selection and placement of war-related photographs, the phrasing of editorials, the acceptance or rejection for publication of "opinion" essays and letters by noted authorities and/or readers, and the approval of political cartoons. A much more obvious way of expressing a pro-Israeli attitude is through the wholesale adoption of the Israeli viewpoint about the invasion. Still a third manner in which Israeli sympathies are manifested is through the frequent use of terms which effectively dehumanize Israel's "enemies," the Palestinians specifically, and all Arabs more generally. This dehumanization tendency is most graphically illustrated in political cartoons which incorporate crude and racist anti-Arab stereotypes.

A pro-Israel tilt can also be observed in the relative paucity of articles dealing with the human consequences of the war. While it is fair to say that reports concentrating on the human dimensions have been regularly published, it is also true that the overwhelming majority of stories have focused upon the political and military aspects of the war....A fifth and final measure of pro-Israeli bias is the implicit -- in certain papers quite explicit -- endorsement of the Israeli invasion that is evident in editorials suggesting that Israel's aggression has, to quote an oft-repeated phrase of the press, "opened opportunities for peace." There is an expressed hope that Israel's actions in Lebanon will lead to positive political results not just for Israel, but also for the United States. And there is undisguised pride that Israel's victories, achieved with the help of American-made weapons, have "proven" the superiority of U.S. technology!...

Basically, the American press has accepted the Israeli position without any serious questioning. What Israel has done has been in the interests of peace! Aggression, invasion of a sovereign country, the violation of international law, these are not considered to be relevant concerns with respect to the situation in Lebanon....According to the New York Times: "Peace is the issue, not Lebanon. There is no Lebanon or plausible plan to revive it. A world that tolerated its disintegration, occupation by Syria and collapse into quasi-feudal baronies, speaks nonsense when it pleads for Lebanese sovereignty or territorial integrity." (June 7, 1982)

Thus, the issue becomes in the American press the same issue as stated by the Israeli government: the right to self-defense, that is, peace and security for

Israel. Indeed, newspaper editors have been quite blunt
on this point since the inception of the invasion on
June 6. For example, the Washington Post...said on June
7: "Unquestionably, the Israelis have a right to
protect their people. The British have just gone 8,000
miles to assert that same principle. Many observers,
including the Reagan administration, had understood
that Israel could not be expected to let its border
towns be indiscriminately shelled...." (June 7, 1982)

According to the Chicago Tribune: "...Israel has
been under attack. Its foe is intransigent and
unrelenting...Israel's justifiable desires to guarantee
its citizens a simple measure of security and to send
its diplomats in peace to foreign capitals has been
repeatedly flouted." (June 8, 1981)

What is so disturbing about the press acceptance
of the Israeli position is the deliberate ignoring of
facts. The Israeli premises are simply untrue. There
was no provocation of Israel as far as shelling of its
towns in the Galilee are concerned. Since July 1981,
when a cease-fire, negotiated through the mediation of
Philip Habib acting as President Reagan's special
envoy, went into effect, the PLO had strictly observed
the terms. It has been Israel which has repeatedly
violated the terms of the U.S. sponsored cease-fire
agreement. This was recognized by Anthony Lewis, the
New York Times columnist whose regular "Abroad at Home"
editorial is syndicated in many newspapers:

> In terms of keeping northern Israel free
> of artillery attacks, that arrangement
> (cease-fire) has been astonishingly
> successful.
> For nine months not a single rocket or
> shell was fired by PLO gunners into Israel.
> When Israeli planes bombed Lebanon on April
> 21 for the first time since the truce
> started, the PLO did not respond. When there
> was another bombing on May 9, there was a
> limited response: about 100 rockets that
> Israel said caused no damage or casualties.
> Then, after the massive Israeli bombing last
> week the PLO responded with full-scale
> barrages.
> In short, the cease-fire kept the
> Galilee safe until Israel bombed Lebanon.
> (June 7, 1982)

Anthony Lewis is not exceptional in his
presentation of the facts, but writers like him are
rare and their ability to impart accurate knowledge of
the facts to editors would appear to be virtually
non-existent. There is a blind acceptance of the

Israeli line which filters out any information which may be contradictory. This can be seen in the general press treatment of the set of events which led to the invasion, the attempted assassination of an Israeli diplomat in London, up to all the incidents which have marked the Israeli besieging and blockade of Beirut since mid-June. For example, when Israel accused the PLO of being responsible for the assassination attempt and initiated massive bombing raids in Lebanon as a retaliation, no newspaper headlined -- or even discussed -- the PLO denial and denunciation of this action. In contrast there were banner headlines about Israel's accusations which were presented as if they were factual statements. Similarly, throughout the prolonged siege of Beirut there have been periods during which Israel has cut off all food, water and electricity, presumably to induce the residents of the western and southern sectors of the city to flee, but these essentially inhumane moves which are in violation of the Geneva accords are only referred to with the briefest of sentences within the text of an article dealing with other matters....

The press has never described Israel's bombing and shelling of Lebanese cities and towns as terrorist acts. Yet, in 1978, 1979, 1980, and 1981 several hundreds of people, more than half of them women and children, were killed in Lebanon as a result of Israeli attacks....

The ultimate dehumanization of the Palestinians has occurred with virtually complete silence in the press -- the Christian Science Monitor is a notable exception -- regarding Israeli treatment of Palestinian prisoners and civilians. The former, numbering as many as 9,000, are being held in internment camps to which Israel has forbidden all press access and for whom Israel refuses to grant the international protections normally extended to POWs....This inhumane policy has not been deemed an appropriate topic of investigation by any of the major metropolitan newspapers. This silence is only explicable when it is realized that the years of describing Palestinians as terrorists has numbed many editors and journalists to the fate of these "sub-human" people.

The insensitivity of the press is not only reflected in prose. It can also be observed visually in the political cartoons....These cartoons employ the crudest of racist stereotypes to depict the Palestinians. Such caricatures would be simply unacceptable if drawn of Jews, or blacks or any other ethnic group....

The tone of editorials especially has been offensive to Arabs and Americans of Arabic heritage. Many of the racist stereotypes which pervade the press

accounts are inaccurate and demeaning caricatures of
reality such as: Palestinians are terrorists; Arabs are
Muslim and anti-Christian; Arabs are incompetent
against the westernized Israelis; the war proved the
superiority of American-made weapons; and that military
might can make political right when dealing with
"inferior" peoples....Right now the Palestinians are in
danger of being as brutally treated by the press as by
their Israeli aggressors.

Lebanon Eyewitness: After Years of Occupation,
A Summer of Pain and Untruth
By Martin Peretz

   Much of what you have read in the newspapers and
newsmagazines about the war in Lebanon -- and even more
of what you have seen and heard on television -- is
simply not true. At best, the routine reportorial
fare, to say nothing of editorial or columnists'
commentary, has been wrenched out of context, detached
from history, exaggerated, distorted. Then there are
the deliberate and systematic falsifications:
remarkably little of what has been alleged in various
published protest statements against the Israeli action
in Lebanon is fact. I know; I was there.
   ...All wars hurt, but some wars are conducted
differently from others -- yes, more humanely, and to
more humane purpose. This I argue -- this I saw with
my own eyes -- is Israel's war in Lebanon. It's a war
too complicated to tell about quickly, too taxing by
way of historical understanding for correspondents
armed with a peculiarly American mixture of ignorance,
cynicism, and brashness, who jet from crisis to crisis
-- looking for Vietnam, and, if possible, for
Watergate, too. There is one other factor: a cohort of
journalists in the Middle East -- Jonathan Randal,
William Claiborne, Edward Cody, and Jim Hoagland, all
of The Washington Post, lead the pack -- with a record
to defend. The events in Lebanon prove them wrong,
some of them deceitfully so, and they shape the facts
-- as they want to shape the future -- to disguise the
disservice they've done their readers, which is to say
the disservice they've done the truth and, therefore,
the foreign policy of our country as well....
   The cities were bombed from the air, shelled from
the sea, set upon over the land. These were not, said

a saddened Israeli colonel, manicured attacks. But
neither were they indiscriminate or wholesale; this was
no war against a civilian population, Lebanese or
Palestinian....

You've seen the destroyed areas on television;
you've probably not seen the vast areas adjacent to
them or those five or ten minutes away. In the hills
beyond Sidon and Tyre, toward the interior, the
countryside has been wholly undisturbed....

Representatives of Oxfam and other agencies are
now all over Lebanon, trying to find a way to spend the
money they've raised and are still raising. Some of
them have gotten into squabbles with Israelis over
bureaucratic obstacles put in the way of distributing
supplies. But the truth is that there is no emergency
in basic human needs: food is plentiful and cheap....

What is clear is that Israel's attack was measured
and careful. I was also in Lebanon after "Operation
Litani" in 1978, another Israeli action that was, in my
view, neither measured nor careful....Nothing
comparable could be said about the events of recent
weeks. This time, Lebanese of all persuasions and
origins have expressed -- I heard it myself dozens of
times -- gratification at their liberation from the
PLO.

It is by now certain that the casualties reported
out of southern Lebanon were false....It is just
possible, it may even by likely, that more civilians
were killed in Lebanon by the Syrians alone --
leaving aside the routine homicidal rampages of the various
Palestinian factions and the Lebanese militias -- in
that virtually unnoticed fighting last spring than in
this entire Israeli war, which has riveted so many
influential Americans to their seats of judgement.
There is a certain promiscuity with zeroes in the Arab
world....

The PLO's behavior in the south does not quite fit
the neat image its propagandists convey to the press.
Confiscations, harassments, young people forced into
the militias, schools closed, rapes, molestations,
commandeering of licenses, passports, services,
offices: this was the stuff of everyday life in the web
of the PLO's "state-within-a-state"....

The uproar over Israeli censorship seems to me to
be in part a projection. The press censored itself for
years on Lebanon. It was not brave, but fearful -- as
it has been not brave but fearful at Hama in Syria or
on the frontiers between Iraq and Iran, places where so
many more were killed than in southern Lebanon....

Ombudsman, "And Now, Good News"
By Robert J. McCloskey

The Columbia Journalism Review is out with welcome news for editors who had been reading a lot and enjoying nothing of what was written about their organizations' coverage of the war in Lebanon last summer.

A well-documented and not altogether uncritical appraisal by press observer Roger Morris concludes that "American journalism came to a bloody new war in the Middle East, reported what it saw for the most part fairly and accurately and sometimes brilliantly, provided balanced comment and provoked and absorbed controversy. For performance under fire, readers and viewers could have asked for little more."

This is how you spell relief for news managers who, until now, knew little but Shakespearean "grim and comfortless despair" from months of criticism. At least those at ABC, CBS, NBC, The New York Times, and The Washington Post, whose broadcasts and pages were emphasized in the survey, will savor the judgement. To a lesser extent, coverage by the Los Angeles Times and The Christian Science Monitor was reviewed.

Allegations of bias in Post reporting have been weighed in this space on several occasions. Like others, this newspaper took fire from both sides, the volume and intensity at a more sustained pitch from the Jewish community. In Israel, Mr. Morris notes, The Jerusalem Post characterized American news reporting of the war as "political pornography." More explicit comments registered here are deemed not fit to print.

For all who have tracked this controversy, I commend the CJR article. Mr. Morris addresses the fairness of reportage on four fronts: the historical context and the rationale for Israel's invasion; the extent of Lebanese "welcome" to the Israelis; accuracy in describing "human and physical cost"; and overall balance.

He's a tad more generous to The Post than I was on its coverage of the PLO's status in Lebanon. It wasn't until Aug. 19, more than two months after the invasion, and almost a month after I had recommended it, that the paper gave its readers a comprehensive account. I found the August 19 piece "informative...on the organization and its antecedents," but inadequate on how it was regarded by the Lebanese. Earlier, as is observed by CJR, The Christian Science Monitor and Los Angeles Times had filed "insightful" and "graphic" accounts of "oppression" and "hate" felt by Lebanese toward the PLO.

Mr. Morris' evaluation of the controversies provoked by civilian casualty figures parallels the experience here. Demands to know how many were being killed drove journalists to accept numbers when they became available. Initial high estimates -- 500,000 homeless, 10,000 casualties -- came variously from the International Committee of the Red Cross, PLO and Lebanese "authorities" and were attributed as such. Here, the issue was aggravated by acceptance of an advertisement in June from the "Ad Hoc Committee in Defense of Palestinian and Lebanese Peoples," claiming without attribution 40,000 killed and 700,000 homeless. Critics read this as eagerness by the paper to pillory Israel. <u>Post</u> reporters, meanwhile, were noting carefully Israeli government charges that figures were inflated, also that "there was no independent confirmation of casualty tolls."

The extended siege of Beirut produced what Mr. Morris characterizes as "some of the most provocative segments of the war." He refers to television correspondents particularly. Print reporters were being criticized for misleading and exaggerated reporting about the damage to nonmilitary targets in the city. Mr. Morris details an angry exchange between <u>New York Times</u> reporter Thomas L. Friedman and his editors, who removed the word "indiscriminate" in a story to describe Israeli bombing.

Of little notice elsewhere, Mr. Morris marks "the silence of Capitol Hill politicians on both sides, not to mention the impact of the invasion on close election campaigns starting up as the fighting and media coverage grew most controversial...." Then he says that "most home-front journalists tended to dive for cover along with the politicians."

I know some who might object to those conclusions. For all the rest, news editors will give thanks.

The Journalists' War against Israel: Techniques of Distortion, Disorientation & Disinformation
By Edward Alexander

The scandalous disregard for truth -- and the deplorable lack of self-critical professionalism, once the hallmark of good foreign correspondents -- that has characterized much of the reporting of the War in Lebanon, especially when the reporting emanates from Beirut, calls to mind the allegations made in February

Reprinted by permission of <u>Encounter</u> from the September-October 1982 issue.

of this year by Zeev Chafetz, director of Israel's
Government Press Office. Chafetz charged that
substantial segments of the Western news media -- among
them The New York Times, The Washington Post, the BBC,
and ABC-TV -- follow a double standard in reporting and
commentary on the Arab-Israel conflict because they
fear or respect Arab terror, but take for granted and
abuse the freedom allowed them in Israel's open
society....

Neither ABC-TV nor Jonathan Randal...is a newcomer
to PLO apologetics. But they are only parts of a
larger tendency, one not readily explainable by the
coercion of PLO terrorism, to flout normal standards of
truthfulness in reporting and rationality in
editorialising on Israel....Time Magazine...has carried
on a virtual war against Israel for years....

Certain newspapers, like the Christian Science
Monitor and Washington Post, or programmes like Sixty
Minutes, believe they are performing a journalistic
duty by depicting Israel as the devil's experiment
station, with its capital neither in Jerusalem nor in
Tel Aviv, but in Sodom and Gomorrah. They unceasingly
report so much nastiness, brutality, "inflexibility,"
and fanaticism in Israel that many of their
impressionable readers must marvel at the prodigious
energy which enables so tiny a people to commit so many
Brobdingnagian misdeeds....

The propaganda battle against Israel began with
the invention of the figure of "600,000 homeless
civilians" supposedly issued by the International
Committee of the Red Cross, working with the
Palestinian Red Crescent Society (which happens to be
headed by Yasser Arafat's brother). The figure, a
patent absurdity on the face of it for an area whose
entire population is under 500,000....

The U.S. magazine Newsweek was distressed because
Israel's war against the PLO, instead of destroying the
movement, had "sorely weakened its more moderate
elements." Newsweek feared that if the extremely
moderate Arafat lost charge the PLO "seems likely to
turn...toward terrorism" (July 19).

Six days later David Shipler published in The New
York Times (July 25) a detailed account -- one which
helped to explain why the Israeli invasion was openly
welcomed by all factions in Lebanon except the PLO and
the extreme Left -- of the terror of six years of
living under the PLO. If these gruesome accounts of the
six-year reign of terror in Lebanon by the PLO (and its
hired mercenaries from a half-dozen other countres)
have unsettled the faith of Newsweek in Arafat's
moderation, the magazine has yet to reveal that fact to
its readers....

In Defense of Casualty Pictures on TV
By Ellen Goodman

BOSTON -- Now that the heavy fighting in Beirut is over and the PLO has been shipped off to live in assorted nations, I am left with one lingering image of this war. No, for once, it's not an image I saw on television. It's an image I saw of television....We beam home the pictures of the wounded, the innocent bystanders, the casualties. And the war lovers don't like that.

Ever since Vietnam, we've heard complaints that television news was somehow biased. There were angry accusations that the nightly news fomented the protest movement in the '70s. Now we hear that the camera, simply by filming the uprooted of Beirut, the refuse of war, made a statement against the Israeli artillery.

There were suggestions that it wasn't quite cricket to offer up "features" on the effects of the war on a family, a street, a building, a neighborhood. I even heard that there was something unfair about "human interest" stories on the wounded of the militarized zone, stories giving them names and faces and titles: aunt, son, father.

Well, I agree that television is biased.

To the degree that TV does its job well, tells us the facts of life in a conflict, it is intrinsically anti-war.

It's anti-war because the average person sitting in the living room responds to another human being....War may be impersonal. But introduce us to a single person,...tell us what happened to his or her life -- and we will care. It is our saving grace.

In our war-sophisticated world, we have learned that before we can kill people, we have to dehumanize them. They are no longer human beings but gooks or kikes or animals. It is even easier when we lob missiles from an invisible distance or drop bombs from 15,000 feet at "targets." It's more like an Atari game than a murder. Conversely, the more we humanize people, the more we personalize war, the harder it is to commit.... TV isn't in the war room or the computer room but the hospital room.... There are people who worry that humanizing war will undermine our resolve to wage it. I say, that is our greatest hope.

Excerpts reprinted from The Washington Post, September 14, 1982.

The New Weapon of War is a TV Camera
By Ben Wattenberg

The most important new weapons are light-weight television cameras and television satellites. They have unwittingly made it more difficult for free nations to operate in the real world.... Communist countries can wage long, brutal wars and pay very little for it. It is 2 1/2 years since the Soviets rolled into Afghanistan.... and the nightly news all over the world ignores the conflict. After all, if you can't get television cameras into a country to witness the poison gas, the dead civilians, the maimed children -- then what can you show on television? No access; no horror....

A democracy can wage a quick war if it is on an isolated, faraway island -- which enables it to successfully control the news. [T]here was no contemporaneous television film of the deaths of the British sailors in the icy sea or in melting aluminum ships. No foreign correspondents were allowed with the fleet; censorship was tight. Question: If English television had shown the gore of the war while it was happening, could Margaret Thatcher have kept the political support necessary to finish the war?

On non-islands, democracies can wage only short wars, telling the whole truth, all at once and immediately if the war goes on, if goals change as target of opportunity arise, if the government says something that is not so -- beware of the wrath of the world. Because both Israel and Lebanon host plenty of television crews, because a television journalist can get to the front quickly in a Hertz car, because the censorship is porous -- every bit of the horror that any war produces is in everybody's living room the next day. In war, access equals horror.

The Israelis are complaining bitterly that Israel is unfairly held up to a double standard. Actually, it is more serious than that. The new rules of media warfare establish a double standard for all open societies.

This is important. The use of force and, more important, the threat of the use of force are still key parts of the global geo-political equation. That is sad, but true.

The nature of television news demands that it show whatever horror is available. Our horror is available, our adversaries is not....

Excerpts reprinted from <u>Philadelphia Inquirer</u>, July 8, 1982.

The Media Front: Where Israel Lost in Lebanon
By Milton Viorst

JERUSALEM -- It was a hard summer for Israel's image,
starting with skeptical questions raised by the press
over the invasion of Lebanon in June, culminating with
the accounts of the Beirut massacre in September. At
first, most Israelis were stunned by the world's
criticism and applauded the government's tenacious
efforts to attribute it to the ignorance and bias of
the international press. The government's main target
was American television, recognized as the medium most
crucial to Israel's future, and for months it succeeded
in keeping American TV journalists on the defensive.
But after the killings in the camps, most Israelis had
to acknowledge that the image problem was less in the
media than in Israel itself. Until recently, Israel
hardly knew critical reporting. The international
press had long portrayed it as a land of settlers
making the desert bloom, of brave men fighting for
independence -- as a peace-loving community permanently
on the alert against the terrorism. Over the years,
the world received a regular diet of journalistic
praise of Israel's technology, universities, democracy,
hospitals, arts....Israelis in large numbers criticized
the invasion last June, but most were nonetheless upset
at the world's disapproval of it. They were sure that
Israel was victimized by dark forces, some
carrying typewriters, others clustered behind whirring
TV cameras....So, throughout the summer, the image
apparatus struggled against the world press, and
particularly against the vivid pictures appearing each
night on American television: ruined buildings, maimed
children, the menacing barrels of Israeli guns, and,
after the massacre, the stacks of cadavers. But as all
this appeared willy-nilly on the screen, Israel did
little except complain of misrepresentation. Dov
Ben-Meir, a Labor Party parliamentarian, was more
strident than most in his rhetoric, but his statement
on the Knesset floor was by no means inconsistent with
what I heard over and over again during my visit to
Israel last summer.
     "The worldwide opposition to the war arises from
the fact that the government did not take into account
the third enemy in Lebanon [after the Palestine
Liberation Organization and the Syrians]: the
international communications media.
     "Just as the Vietnam War was decided by none other
than the television cameras, so in this war the TV cam-

Reprinted from Channels, November/December 1982 by
permission of the author.

eras caused us more damage than the combined strength of all our enemies in Lebanon...."

Israelis are as outspoken as any people on earth; out of this Babel emerges a rich and diverse journalism, in which the demands of image constantly clash with the quest for truth. While the Israelis were fighting the PLO in Lebanon, Russians were fighting in Afghanistan, the Iraqis and Iranians in the Persian Gulf, the British and the Argentines in the Falkland Islands. Not only was news from these three war zones almost totally suppressed, but the various audiences at home demanded nothing better. Israelis would never accept such limitations on news, nor would they expect the outside world to accept them.

Thus, in a sense, the Israeli press ran interference for the foreign press. Erwin Frenkel, for instance, shared the government's concern for Israel's good name but as editor of The Jerusalem Post helped provide information used by foreign reporters to criticize the war. From the start, though the government tried to shape Israeli coverage of the conflict -- it won a few victories, particularly over state television and radio....

J'Accuse
By Norman Podhoretz

The war in Lebanon triggered an explosion of invective against Israel that in its fury and its reach was unprecedented in the public discourse of this country. In the past, unambiguously venemous attacks on Israel had been confined to marginal sectors of American political culture like the Village Voice and the Nation on the far Left and their counterparts in such publications of the far Right as the Liberty Lobby's Spotlight. Even when, as began happening with greater and greater frequency after the Six-Day War of 1967, Israel was attacked in more respectable quarters, care was often taken to mute the language or modulate the tone. Usually the attack would be delivered more in sorrow than in anger, and it would be accompanied by sweet protestations of sympathy. The writer would claim to be telling the Israelis harsh truths for their own good as a real friend should, on the evident assumption that he had a better idea than they did of how to insure their security, and even survival. In perhaps the most notable such piece, George W. Ball (of whom more later) explained to the readers of Foreign Affairs "How to Save Israel in Spite of Herself." No

matter that Ball warned the Israelis that unless they
adopted policies they themselves considered too
dangerous, he for one would recommend the adoption of
other policies by the United States that would leave
them naked unto their enemies; no matter that he
thereby gave the Israelis a choice, as they saw it,
between committing suicide and being murdered; he still
represented himself as their loyal friend.

And so it was with a host of other commentators,
including prominent columnists like Anthony Lewis of
the New York Times, academic pundits like Stanley
Hoffmann of Harvard, and former diplomatic
functionaries like Harold Saunders. To others it might
seem that their persistent hectoring of Israel was
making a considerable contribution to the undermining
of Israel's case for American support and thereby
endangering Israel's very existence. Nevertheless,
they would have all the world know that they yielded to
no one in their commitment to the survival of Israel.
Indeed, it was they, and not Israel's "uncritical"
supporters, who were Israel's best friends in this
country. As a matter of fact, they were even better
friends to Israel than most Israelis themselves who,
alas, were their "own worst enemies" (an idea which
recently prompted Conor Cruise O'Brien, the former
editor of the London Observer, to remark: "Well, I
suppose Israelis may be their own worst enemies, but if
they are, they have had to overcome some pretty stiff
competition for that coveted title").

This kind of thing by no means disappeared from
the public prints with the Israeli move into Lebanon.
In the thick file of clippings I have before me there
are many expressions of "anguish" and "sadness" over
the damage Israel was doing to its "image" and to its
"good name." In a fairly typical effusion, Alfred
Friendly wrote in the Washington Post (of which he was
formerly the managing editor):

> Perhaps it was expecting more than was
> possible -- that Israel should remain the
> country with a conscience, a home for honor,
> a treasury for the values of mind and soul.
> At any rate, it is so no longer but merely a
> nation like any other, its unique splendor
> lost....its slaughters are on a par
> with...Trujillo's Dominican Republic or Papa
> Doc's Haiti. Still absent are the jackboots,
> the shoulder boards, and the bemedalled
> chests, but one can see them, figuratively,
> on the minister of defense. No doubt Israel
> is still an interesting country. But not for
> the reasons, the happy reasons, that made it
> such for me.

In addition to lamenting Israel's loss of moral stature as a result of Lebanon, these great friends of Israel condemned the resort to "unselective and disproportionate violence" (Anthony Lewis) on the ground that it "cannot serve the spirit of Israel, or its true security."

But the sympathetic protestations of this particular species of friend -- including Lewis, perhaps the most unctious of them all -- became more perfunctory and more mechanical in the weeks after the war began. One got the feeling that they were offered mainly for the record or to fend off criticism. And in any case, the preponderant emphasis was no longer on the putative damage Israel was doing to itself by its wicked or stupid policies. The focus was now mistakably on the evils Israel was committing against others, as in this passage from a column by Richard Cohen in the Washington Post:

> Maybe the ultimate tragedy of the seemingly nonstop war in the Middle East is that Israel has adopted the morality of its hostile neighbors. Now it bombs cities, killing combatants and non-combatants alike -- men as well as women, women as well as children, Palestinians as well as Lebanese.

Israel's "true friends," then, were liberated by Lebanon to say much more straightforwardly and in more intemperate terms than before what they had all along felt: that Israeli intransigence and/or aggressiveness and/or expansionism are the main (and for some, the only) source of the Arab-Israeli conflict and therefore the main (or only) obstacle to a peaceful resolution of that conflict.

Even if this were all, it would have increased the volume and intensity of the attacks on Israel to an unprecedented level. But what made matters much worse was the proportionate escalation and increasing respectability of the attacks from quarters that had never pretended to friendly concern with Israel.

To be sure, apologists for the PLO who had always been ugly about Israel -- Edward Said, Alexander Cockburn, and Nicholas von Hoffman, to mention three prominent names -- had been getting a more and more deferential hearing in recent years. Books by Said like The Question of Palestine have been widely and sympathetically reviewed in the very media he indiscriminately denounces for being anti-Arab; Cockburn, whose weekly pieces in the Village Voice have set a new standard of gutter journalism in this country (and not merely in dealing with Israel), has been rewarded with regular columns in <u>Harper's</u> and the <u>Wall Street Journal</u> (where in exchange for access to a respectable middle-class audience he watches his literary manners); and von Hoffman, who is only slightly less scurrilous than Cockburn, has also found a hospitable welcome in <u>Harper's</u> and a host of other mainstream periodicals both here and abroad (not to mention the television networks). Writing to a British audience in the <u>London Spectator</u> (for which he does a regular column), [Nicholas] von Hoffman exulted openly in this change:

> Where before it was difficult to print or say something that was critical of Israeli policies and practices, the barriers are now coming down. Some writers used to believe -- rightly or wrongly -- that to expound a Palestinian view was to risk blacklisting. Now many have become emboldened....

But if they were becoming "emboldened" before Lebanon, their tongues now lost all restraint. Von Hoffman himself is a case in point, having been emboldened in another piece in the <u>Spectator</u> to compare Lebanon to Lidice and the Israelis to the Nazis: "Incident by incident, atrocity by atrocity, Americans are coming to see the Israel government as pounding the Star of David into a swastika."

Whether von Hoffman published these words in the United States, I do not know, but by his own account he could easily have found an outlet. "Where once, among the daily press, only the <u>Boston Globe</u> could be counted on to print other points of view as a matter of consistent policy...now other voices are becoming somewhat more audible."

Somewhat? According to one estimate, of the first 19 pieces on the war in Lebanon to appear on the <u>New York Times</u> Op-Ed page, 17 were hostile to Israel and only two (one of them by me) were sympathetic. I have not made a statistical survey of the <u>Washington Post</u> Op-Ed page, but my impression is that the balance there was roughly the same. In short, not only did the kind of virulent pieces formerly confined to the <u>Village Voice</u> and other yellow journals of the Left and Right increase in number and intensity; such pieces now also began appearing regularly in reputable papers and magazines.

Thus no sooner had the Israelis set foot in Lebanon than Edward Said was to be found on the Op-Ed page of the <u>New York Times</u> declaring that Sidon and Tyre had been "laid waste, their civilian inhabitants killed or made destitute by Israeli carpet bombing," and accusing Israel of pursuing "an apocalyptic logic

of exterminism." The comparison of Israel with the
Nazis here was less brazen than in von Hoffman's piece,
but William Pfaff more than made up for it in the
International Herald Tribune: "Hitler's work goes on,"
he began, and concluded with the prediction that Hitler
might soon "find rest in Hell" through "the knowledge
that the Jews themselves, in Israel, have finally
...accepted his own way of looking at things." The
famous spy novelist John le Carre was imported from
England by the Boston Globe to deliver himself of
similar sentiments:

> Too many Israelis, in their
> claustrophobia, have persuaded themselves
> that every Palestinian man and woman and
> child is by definition a military target, and
> that Israel will not be safe until the pack
> of them are swept away. It is the most
> savage irony that Begin and his generals
> cannot see how close they are to inflicting
> upon another people the disgraceful criteria
> once inflicted upon themselves.

Finally, the syndicated cartoonist Oliphant, like
Cockburn in the Wall Street Journal, portrayed besieged
west Beirut as another Warsaw ghetto, with the PLO in
the role of the Jews and the Israelis in the role of
the Nazis.
   Many other writers were also "emboldened" by
Lebanon, but not quite enough to compare the Israelis
with the Nazis. Alfred Friendly, in the passage quoted
above, only compared them to Trujillo and Duvalier.
Hodding Carter, in the Wall Street Journal, invoked
Sparta (though his use of language like "Several
Lebanese towns have been pulverized by the tactics of
total war [and] tens of thousands of Lebanese have been
killed or injured since the blitzkrieg was launched"
suggested that Sparta was not really the state he had
in mind). And Joseph C. Harsch, in the Christian
Science Monitor, brought up Communist Vietnam: "Vietnam
is imperial. It dominate[s] its neighbors Laos and
Cambodia. In that same sense Israel is now the dominant
power in its own area." Extending this ingenious
comparison, Harsch wrote:

> Israel's major weapons come from the
> U.S. Israel's economy is sustained by
> subsidies from the U.S.....It depends on
> Washington, just as Vietnam depends for major
> arms and for economic survival on Moscow.
> Neither Israel nor Vietnam could dominate
> their neighborhoods if the support of their
> major partrons were withdrawn.

But the prize for the most startling comparison of all goes to Mary McGrory of the <u>Washington Post</u>, who was reminded of the dropping of atomic bombs on Hiroshima and Nagasaki. More startling still, Miss McGrory said that in her opinion what the Israelis were doing in Lebanon was worse. Addressing Begin directly she wrote:

> You were trying to save your own troops. We understand that. We are, after all, the country that dropped atomic bombs on Hiroshima and Nagasaki....But grant us that we were up against a mighty, if weakened, war machine and a totally mobilized nation. You were punishing a wretched country that reluctantly shelters factions, which, while hostile to you, could not wipe you off the face of the earth, however much they might want to.

What are we to make of words and images like these? How are we to explain them? How are we to understand what they portend?

There are well-wishers of Israel, among them a number of Jews, who recoil in horror from the idea that the Israelis are no better than Nazis, but who believe that Israel under Menachem Begin and Ariel Sharon has brought all this violent abuse on itself. Even though the degree of condemnation is excessive, say these anxious well-wishers, the Israelis have only themselves to blame for besmirching their "good name." Yet I would suggest that the beginning of wisdom in thinking about this issue is to recognize that the vilification of Israel is the phenomenon to be addressed, and not the Israeli behavior that supposedly provoked it. I say supposedly because when a reaction is as wildly disproportionate to an event as this one was, it is clearly being fed by sources other than the event itself.

But what am I or anyone else to say to those for whom there is nothing obvious about the assertion that in this particular case the reaction was disproportionate? From such people one is tempted to turn away in disgust. Yet difficult as it may be to entertain, even for as long as it takes to refute it, the loathsome idea that Israel is to the Palestinians as the Nazis were to the Jews, the world evidently still needs to be reminded of the differences.

To begin with, then, the Nazis set out to murder every Jew on the face of the earth, and wherever they had the power to do so, they systematically pursued this objective. Is this what the Israelis have tried to do to the Palestinians? If so, they have gone about it in a most peculiar way.

In Germany under the Nazis, the Jews were first stripped of their civil and political rights and then sent to concentration camps where virtually all of them were put to death. For more than thirty-five years, by contrast, Palestinian Arabs living in the state of Israel have enjoyed Israeli citizenship and along with it a degree of civil and political liberty, not to mention prosperity, unknown to Arabs living in any country under Arab sovereignty.

For fifteen years, moreover, about a million Palestinians on the West Bank and Gaza have been in the power of Israel under military occupation. Have squads of gunmen been dispatched to shoot them down in the fashion of the _Einsatzgruppen_ who murdered an approximately equal number of Jews in those parts of the Soviet Union occupied by the Nazis? Have the West Bank Palestinians been rounded up and deported to concentration camps in preparation for being gassed, as happened to some three million Jews living in other countries occupied by Nazi Germany? The Nazis in less than six years managed to kill more than five million Jews in occupied territory. How many Palestinian Arabs have been killed by the Israelis in fifteen years? A hundred? And if even that many, has a single civilian been killed as a matter of policy? Again, the fact is that the Palestinians living under military occupation, and even since the recent political offensive against PLO influence on the West Bank, have enjoyed a greater degree of civil and political liberty than any of their brother Arabs living anywhere else except in Israel as Israeli citizens.

It is or ought to be obvious, then, that any comparison between the way Israel has treated the Palestinians and the way the Nazis dealt with the Jews is from a rational perspective, let alone morally, disproportionate to a monstrous degree. Anyone who makes such a comparison cannot possibly be responding to the facts of the case and must be driven by some other impulse.

But what about the comparisons of Israel with Sparta, or Haiti, or Communist Vietnam? Are they any the less disproportionate? If so, it is only because nothing could match the intellectual and moral excess of equating Jews with Nazis. Still, these comparisons are sufficiently outlandish in their own right.

Sparta, to start with the least repellent of them, was a police state so dedicated to war and so singlemindedly devoted to the martial values that any male child deemed unfit to become a soldier was taken to the mountains and abandoned to his death. Israel is a democracy with an army made up largely of civilian reservists to whom nothing is more distasteful than going to war and to whom peace is the highest value. As for Haiti or the Dominican Republic under Trujillo, they have so little in common with Israel in any respect that bringing their names into the discussion can only be seen as an effort to sneak by with the absurd charge that Israel is no longer a democratic country.

Apparently, though, not even this charge was too absurd to surface openly in the public prints. Thus, Douglas S. Crow, Professor of Religion, no less, at Columbia University, wrote in a letter to the New York Times of Israel's "posturing as a bastion of democracy." But if Israel, where all citizens, including Arabs, have the right to vote and where all individuals and parties, including the Communists, enjoy a full range of liberties -- speech, press, assembly, and so on -- is not a bastion of democracy, where shall such a bastion be found?

The same point can be made of the analogy with Communist Vietnam, where there is even greater repression than in Trujillo's Dominican Republic and perhaps even greater economic misery than in Haiti. To compare Israel -- which can indeed be described as a bastion of democracy -- with what is by all accounts one of the most Stalinist regimes in the entire Communist world, is a sufficiently gross travesty. But is the comparison Joseph C. Harsch makes between the behavior of the two states toward their respective neighbors any more justifiable?

Both, says Mr. Harsch, are "imperial" states using military forces to dominate the countries of the region. That this is an apt characterization of Communist Vietnam very few will nowadays contest. Two years after signing a peace treaty with South Vietnam, the Communist regime of the North invaded and conquered the South. Not content with that, Vietnam proceeded to invade Cambodia where it installed another puppet regime, while keeping some 40,000 troops in Laos to insure its domination over the Communist regime there. Nor could Vietnam claim to be acting defensively: neither South Vietnam nor Cambodia nor Laos posed any threat to Hanoi.

If we now ask what this set of relationships has in common with the relations between Israel and its neighbors, the answer can only be: nothing whatever. One grows weary of reciting the facts of the Arab-Israeli conflict over and over again. But the controversy generated by Lebanon demonstrates that far from being tiresomely familiar, they are still unknown by some and forgotten or deliberately ignored by others for whom they are politically convenient.

In 1947, then, the United Nations adopted a

partition plan for Palestine, dividing it into a Jewish
state and a Palestinian one. The Jews accepted the
plan; the Arabs rejected it. The form this rejection
took was a war against the new Jewish state of Israel
launched by the armies of five neighboring Arab states,
with the aid and encouragement of all the others.
Israel successfully fended off this assault and begged
its neighbors to make peace with it. But they all
refused, rededicating themselves instead to the
elimination of any trace of a sovereign Jewish state
from the region.

Living in consequence under siege, with a
coalition of nineteen nations pledged to its
destruction, Israel maneuvered as best it could. In
1956, it joined forces with the British and the French
in an attack on Egypt which left the Israelis in
control of a stretch of the Sinai desert. But in
response to American pressure, all three parties soon
withdrew, and Israel in particular returned the Sinai
to Egypt (without any quid pro quo). So much for the
first instance of Israeli "expansionism" or
"imperialism" and the only one to which these epithets
have so much as a remotely plausible claim.

The next episode occurred in 1967, when Egypt took
a series of actions clearly spelling an intention to
resort once again to military force whose explicit
objective was -- as its then leader, Nasser, put it --
"the destruction of Israel." After waiting for about
two weeks while the United States and others worked
unsuccessfully to avert a war in which they might be
"wiped off the map" (Nasser's language again) if the
Arabs struck the first blow, the Israelis launched a
preemptive attack. Six days later, thanks to a
brilliant campaign, they found themselves in possession
of territory formerly belonging to or occupied by Egypt
(the Sinai), Syria (the Golan Heights), and Jordan (the
West Bank).

To other Arabs and their apologists, this was
another instance of expansionism and imperialism. But
since virtually no one doubts that Nasser provoked the
1967 war or believes that there would have been a war
at all if not for his closing of the Straits of Tiran
(among other actions he took), how can it be regarded
as an imperialistic operation by Israel? In any case,
Israel begged King Hussein of Jordan to stay out of the
war once it started, and if he had agreed, the Israelis
would not have been obliged to respond to his attack
and they would not have ended the war in control of the
West Bank.

Even so, Israel once again, as it had been doing
since the day of its birth, asked only for recognition
and face-to-face negotiations with its Arab neighbors.
Such negotiations would have resulted in the return of

occupied territories with whatever minor boundary
adjustments security might dictate. Yet once again, as
they had from the beginning, the Arab states refused,
responding this time with the famous three No's of
Khartoum: No recognition, No negotiation, No peace.

Finally, seven years later and after yet another
war -- this one unambiguously started by Egypt in a
surprise attack -- Anwar Sadat (Nasser's successor)
called what had been universally regarded in the Arab
world as Israel's "bluff" by offering recognition and
face-to-face negotiations. Almost overnight, Israel
responded by agreeing to return every inch of Egyptian
territory and then honored the agreement. So much for
imperialism.

Now comes Lebanon. To show that Israel is behaving
toward Lebanon as Vietnam has behaved toward Cambodia,
Joseph C. Harsch writes:

> Israel has now decreed that there must
> be no more "foreign" military forces in
> Lebanon. That means that Israel wants all
> Palestinian and Syrian armed units out of
> Lebanon, leaving Lebanon in the hands of
> elements which would be sympathetic to Israel
> and to its interests.

There are so many astonishing features in these
two sentences that one hardly knows where to begin. In
the first place, why the quotation marks around the
word foreign? Is Harsch trying to suggest that the
"Palestinian and Syrian armed units" are indigenous or
native to Lebanon? In the second place, what is
illegitimate about Israel's desire to leave Lebanon "in
the hands of elements which would be sympathetic to
Israel and its interests"? In view of the fact that
those "elements" would be the Lebanese people
themselves, there can be nothing wrong in leaving
Lebanon in their hands; and in view of the fact that
before Lebanon was taken over by the PLO and the
Syrians it was sufficiently "sympathetic to Israel and
its interests" to live peacefully alongside Israel, a
more accurate way of putting the case would be to say
that Israel hopes to free Lebanon from the domination
of foreign forces who have turned an unwilling Lebanon
into a battlefield of their war against Israel.

But of course putting it that way would defeat the
purpose of portraying Israel as an imperialistic power
imposing its will upon a helpless neighbor. And it
would also show the falsity of describing the war as an
invasion of Lebanon. Yes, the Israelis did invade
Lebanon in the sense of sending military forces across
the Lebanese border. But if we are looking for
analogies, a better one than any fished up in recent

weeks would be the invasion of France by allied troops in World War II. The purpose was not to conquer France but to liberate it from its German conquerors, just as the purpose of the Israelis in 1982 was to liberate Lebanon from the PLO.

Harsch and many of his colleagues may not know this, but the Lebanese people do. In spite of the sufferings inflicted upon them by the war, and in spite of the fact that they have no love for Israel, they have greeted the Israelis as liberators. Representative Charles Wilson, a Texas Democrat who is so far from being reflexively pro-Israel that he voted for the AWACS sale and intends to vote for the Jordanian arms sale, testified after a visit to Lebanon in July to

> the universal enthusiasm with which the Lebanese welcomed the Israeli army....I mean it's almost like a liberating army....It was astonishing. I expected this, somewhat, from the Christian population. But I didn't expect it from the Muslim population....And in talking to a group of people, some of whom had lost their homes, some of whom had lost relatives, they said it was awful. But they said that all in all, to be free of the PLO it was worth it.

Once can see why. According to a news story by David K. Shipler in the New York Times, the PLO, whose "major tool of persuasion was the gun," ruled over a large part of Lebanon, terrifying and terrorizing the local populace, Christian and Muslim alike. It took over land and houses, it confiscated automobiles, it stole at will from the shops, and anyone who complained was likely to be shot. Operating as a state within a state, the PLO humiliated local Lebanese officials and displaced them with its own police and "people's committees."

On top of all this, writes Shipler, the PLO "brought mercenaries in from Bangladesh, Sri Lanka, Pakistan, and North African countries. By all accounts the outsiders were crude, undisciplined thugs." And then there were the killings. "Before the PLO," one Lebanese woman told Shipler, "we used to be pro-Palestinian....[But] when we saw the Palestinians were killing us and threatening us and having barricades and shooting innocent people, then came the hatred."

Rowland Evans and Robert Novak, whose column has always been notorious for its pro-Arab bias, arrived at the same assessment: "Once incorruptible, its extraordinary success in accumulating arms and money...had made the PLO itself an occupying power...permeated by thugs and adventurers."

If this disposes of the idea that a Vietnam-like Israel was imposing its imperial will upon Lebanon, it does not dispose of the charge that the war in Lebanon was imperialistic in a different sense -- that Israel's purpose, as Anthony Lewis (among many others) charges, was "to exterminate Palestinian nationalism" in preparation for annexing the West Bank.

Here again, before taking up the substance, one is forced to begin by pointing to the form in which the charge is expressed. By using the word "exterminate" -- a word which is inescapably associated with what the Nazis did to the Jews -- Lewis contrives to evoke the comparison while covering himself by designating "Palestinian nationalism" rather than Palestinian people as the victim. But even in this form the charge is an outlandish misrepresentation. For the maximum objective of the Begin government is to establish Israeli sovereignty in the West Bank while allowing to the Palestinians living there a degree of control over their own civil and political affairs far greater -- once more the point must be stressed -- than they have ever enjoyed in the past, or than Arabs enjoy in any country under Arab sovereignty. This is "to exterminate Palestinian nationalism"?

And even this -- to repeat, Begin's maximum objective -- is subject by Begin's own commitment to negotiation. That is, in signing the Camp David agreement, Begin has obligated the state of Israel to settle the question of sovereignty after five years by negotiations among all the interested parties, including the West Bank Palestinians. This means that whether Begin and Sharon like it or not, they or their successors might well find themselves turning over the West Bank to Jordan or to a new Palestinian leadership willing, unlike the PLO, to live in peace both with Israel and Jordan.

It is precisely the hope of encouraging such a leadership to emerge that lies behind the two-sided strategy of destroying the PLO as a military force in Lebanon and as a political force on the West Bank. I urge anyone who doubts this to read "How to Make Peace with the Palestinians" by Menahem Milson (Commentary, May 1981). In that article Milson said that Israeli policy on the West Bank had in the past inadvertently led to the strengthening of the PLO's influence there. He therefore advocated a new policy aimed at weakening the PLO so that the "silenced majority" -- which in his judgment wished to live in peace with Israel -- could make itself heard. The end result was to be a demand by the Palestinians on the West Bank that King Hussein repudiate the PLO as "the sole representative of the

Palestinian people" and resume his old role as their spokesman.

After reading that article, Begin and Sharon appointed Milson (then a professor of Arabic literature at the Hebrew University) to the post of civil administrator of the West Bank, from which position he has been putting the policy outlined in the article into practice. The PLO and its apologists have naturally done everything in their power to sabotage and discredit Milson. But the political war against the PLO was proceeding on the West Bank as the military campaign against the PLO in Lebanon was being launched.

No one can say what the eventual disposition of the West Bank will be. What one can say with complete assurance, however, is that so long as the only alternative to Israeli occupation is a Palestinian state ruled over by radical forces pledged to the destruction of Israel, then no Israeli government -- no matter who might be its prime minister -- will be permitted by Israeli public opinion to withdraw. But one can also say, though with less assurance, that if an alternative should present itself, then no Israeli government, including one headed by Ariel Sharon, would be permitted by Israeli public opinion to absorb the West Bank.

But whatever their motives, many or (as I read Israeli public opinion) most Israelis would favor a withdrawal from the West Bank provided they were reasonably confident that the successor regime would be willing to live in peace with a neighboring Jewish state (and provided also, probably, that Jews who wished to go on living in Judea and Samaria would have the same right to do so as Arabs have in Israel). Elimination of the radical rejectionist Palestinians -- whether or not they call themselves the PLO -- is a precondition for any such resolution of the Palestinian problem. Consequently if Begin and Sharon succeed in their objective of destroying the PLO, they may well make it impossibly difficult for Israel to annex or absorb the West Bank -- not because of pressures coming from Washington but because of pressures coming from within Israel itself.

All this, however, is for the future. Returning to the present and to the war in Lebanon we still have to face the charge that Israel was waging a wanton and indiscriminate campaign against defenseless civilians.

In the early days of the war, words like "holocaust" and even "genocide" freely circulated in the media, along with horrendous estimates of the number of civilians killed or rendered homeless by Israeli arms. At first it was said that 10,000 people had been "slaughtered" in southern Lebanon and 600,000 turned into refugees. But no sooner had these figures been imprinted on the public mind than it was revealed that the local Lebanese authorities themselves put the total population of the area in question at 510,000 -- almost 100,000 fewer than were supposedly driven out of their homes. Israel claimed that there were 20,000 refugees and perhaps 2,000 casualties, of whom more than half were only wounded. Correspondents and other visitors to Lebanon soon confirmed that the original figures were "extreme exaggerations" (Shipler), while casting evenhanded doubt on the much lower Israeli figures. Even though "discussions with local officials and residents of the cities tend to reinforce the Israeli estimates of casualties there," wrote Shipler, "the Israeli figures exclude a lot."

Thus arose what came to be called "the numbers game." But the damage to Israel had already been done. In any case, what did it matter, asked Mary McGrory, what the exact figures were? Whatever the precise number, "It is already too many." In her open letter to Begin, she asked:

> Does Israel's security have to be purchased by the slaughter of innocents?...We have been seeing every night pictures of wounded babies and old men. We read about people standing outside devastated apartment buildings, wearing masks against the stench of corpses, waiting to go in to claim their dead. They were a threat to you? Yes, we know, your planes dropped leaflets before they dropped the bombs. But why did you have to bomb their cities at all? People in apartment buildings may be PLO sympathizers or even devoted adherents of Yasir Arafat. But they were unarmed civilians.

Indeed they were, but Miss McGrory's letter might better have been directed to Arafat than to Begin. For (in Shipler's words):

> The huge sums of money the PLO received from Saudi Arabia and other Arab countries seem to have been spent primarily on weapons and ammunition, which were placed strategically in densely populated civilian areas in the hope that this would either deter Israeli attacks or exact a price from Israel in world opinion for killing civilians. Towns and camps were turned into vast armories as crates of ammunition were stacked in underground shelters and antiaircraft guns were emplaced in

schoolyards, among apartment houses, next to churches and hospitals. The remains could be seen soon after the fighting, and Palestinians and Lebanese can still point out the sites.

This strategy of hiding behind civilians was entirely natural for the terrorist organization whose greatest exploits in the past invariably involved hijackings and the killing of innocent bystanders. Having held airplanes and buildings hostage, the PLO -- as the American Lebanese League declared in a newspaper advertisement -- was now holding much of Lebanon itself hostage, and especially west Beirut. Who, the League asked, gave "the PLO authority to insist that Lebanese civilians die with them?" Certainly not the Lebanese civilians themselves.

It is also important to note that under international law (specifically Article 28 of the Geneva Convention of 1948), "the presence of a protected person may not be used to render certain points or areas immune from military operations," and the responsibility for civilian casualties or damage rests on the party, in this case the PLO, who thus uses protected persons or areas. What the other side, in this instance Israel, is required to do is exactly the kind of thing Miss McGrory derides in her reference to the dropping of leaflets: that is, warn the civilians so that they have a chance to leave the area or otherwise protect themselves.

While scrupulously observing this requirement, the Israelis also took other steps to minimize civilian casualties, some of which led to an increase in their own casualties. This is why Miss McGrory's citation of the bombing of Hiroshima and Nagasaki is so bizarre. As it happens, I myself agree with her in thinking that the United States was justified in that action (because the result was to shorten the war and to save many more lives than were lost in the two raids). But the whole point of the bombing of Hiroshima and Nagasaki was to wreak indiscriminate damage which would terrorize the Japanese into surrendering. The Israelis were doing almost exactly the opposite in Lebanon. Their strikes were so careful and discriminating that whole areas of southern Lebanon were left untouched. If they really had been carpet bombing, both the levels of destruction and the number of casualties would have been far greater.

That a left-wing liberal like Mary McGrory should be driven into comparing Israel's military tactics in Lebanon with the dropping of the atom bomb on Hiroshima and Nagasaki is demented enough. But that she should go on to defend the use of the atom bomb by the United

States (which in any other context she would surely
condemn) in order to score an invidious point against
Israel is a measure of how far her animus extends. It
literally knows no bounds.

Obviously a reaction like this can no more have
been provoked by the facts of Israel's behavior than
the comparisons of Israel with Nazi Germany. Nor can
the relatively milder denunciations of Israel as
comparable to Sparta or Haiti or Vietnam be taken as a
rational response to what Israel has done. What then
can explain them?

In thinking about this question while reading
through dozens of vitriolic attacks on Israel, I have
resisted the answer that nevertheless leaps
irresistibly into the mind. This answer, of course, is
that we are dealing here with an eruption of
anti-Semitism. I have resisted because I believe that
loose or promiscuous use of the term anti-Semitism can
only rob it of force and meaning (which is what has
happened to the term racism). In my judgment,
therefore, it should be invoked only when the case for
doing so is clear and precise. When that condition is
met, however, I also believe that one has a duty to
call the offending idea by its proper name.

Not everyone agrees, not even Meg Greenfield, who
in _Newsweek_ happily endorses "plain talk about Israel"
and who as editor of the _Washington Post_ editorial page
has certainly done a lot of plain talking herself.
Miss Greenfield sees it as a "good thing" that the
"resentful, frustrated, expedient silences" Americans
have maintained over Israel have now been "interrupted
by outraged, emotional condemnations of what Israel is
doing." Some of this, she acknowledges, is excessive:
"The comparison [of the Israeli invasion] to Nazi
policy, for instance, has been as disproportionate in
its way as the military violence it complains of." But
the rest is understandable, and is anyway not to be
confused with being anti-Israel or anti-Semitic.
Indeed these very accusations have intensified the
pent-up resentments which are now exploding into what
Miss Greenfield calls "no-holds-barred attacks on the
Israeli action."

In other words, though we are to have "plain talk
about Israel," and though such talk is healthy when
directed against Israel, we are not to have equally
plain talk about the attacks on Israel. To say that
such "no-holds-barred attacks on Israel" are
anti-Israel is unhealthy, and to say that they are
anti-Semitic is even worse.

George W. Ball also rules out any use of the term
anti-Semitism:

I long ago made it a practice not to

answer any letter questioning my position on
Middle East problems that contains the
assertion or implication that I have said or
written anything anti-Semitic. That
accusation, in my view, is a denial -- I
might even say an evasion -- of rational
argument.

Yet when he goes on to explain why it is absurd to
accuse him of anti-Semitism, he brings forth so shallow
a conception of what the term means that it can only be
described as historically illiterate. Anti-Semitism,
according to Ball, is the dislike of Jews; it is
therefore a sufficient refutation to point out that
some of his best friends are Jewish, and that all his
life he has admired the Jews for their contribution to
the arts, to intellectual life, and to liberal causes.
That a man of George Ball's experience and
education should regard this as an adequate account of
anti-Semitism reveals an astonishing blind spot. But
this blindness is an advantage, enabling Ball to accuse
American Jews of dual loyalty -- a classic anti-Semitic
canard that also surfaced in the debate over AWACS --
and then indignantly and self-righteously to deny that
this makes him an anti-Semite.
Unlike Ball, Conor Cruise O'Brien, who has a habit
of speaking plainly on all subjects, does believe that
some critics of Israel are "motivated by some kind of
anti-Semitic feeling, possibly unconscious." In some
instances, he concedes, it may be that what is at work
is "genuine compassion for suffering Arabs, expressing
itself in terms of a generous hyperbole." But in most
others "there are indications to the contrary." These
indications include the absence of any concern for the
civilian casualties in the war between Iraq and Iran,
and the silence that greeted the killing of an
estimated 20,000 Sunni Muslims recently by President
Assad of Syria in the city of Hama. (To O'Brien's
examples may be added the indifference to the 100,000
people killed in internecine strife in Lebanon since
1975 on the part of virtually all those who have wept
over the civilian casualties in Lebanon since the
Israelis went in.) O'Brien suggests, however, that a
term other than anti-Semitic is needed because "the
people in question are...extravagantly philo-Semitic
these days, in their feelings for the Arabic-speaking
branch of the Semitic linguistic family." He proposes
"anti-Jewism," and he offers a test by which it can be
detected in the discussion of Israel: "If your
interlocutor can't keep Hitler out of the conversation,
...feverishly turning Jews into Nazis and Arabs into
Jews -- why then I think, you may well be talking to an
anti-Jewist."

The trouble is that the term "anti-Jewist" cannot be applied to those like George Ball who are loud in their protestations of friendship for the Jewish people, and who might even agree that comparing the Israelis with the Nazis deserves to be called anti-Semitic.

Let me therefore propose that we retain the historically sanctioned term anti-Semitism and let me outline a more general criterion for identifying it than the one O'Brien suggests. Historically anti-Semitism has taken the form of labeling certain vices and failings as specifically Jewish when they are in fact common to all humanity: Jews are greedy, Jews are tricky, Jews are ambitious, Jews are clannish -- as though Jews were uniquely or disproportionately guilty of all those sins. Correlatively, Jews are condemned when they claim or exercise the right to do things that all other people are accorded an unchallengeable right to do.

As applied to the Jewish state, this tradition has been transmuted into the double standard by which Israel is invariably judged. The most egregious illustration is the UN resolution condemning Zionism as a form of racism. According to the thinking of this resolution, all other people are entitled to national self-determination, but when the Jews exercise this right, they are committing the crimes of racism and imperialism. Similarly, all other nations have a right to insure the security of their borders; when Israel exercises this right, it is committing the crime of aggression. So too, only Israel of all the states in the world is required to prove that its very existence -- not merely its interests or the security of its borders, but its very existence -- is in immediate peril before it can justify the resort to force. For example, whereas the possibility of a future threat to its borders was (rightly in my opinion) deemed a sufficient justification by the United States under John F. Kennedy to go to the brink of nuclear war in the Cuban missile crisis of 1962, the immense caches of arms discovered in PLO dumps in southern Lebanon have not persuaded many of the very people who participated in or applauded Kennedy's decision that the Israelis were at least equally justfied in taking action against the PLO in Lebanon.

Criticisms of Israel based on a double standard deserve to be called anti-Semitic. Conversely criticisms of Israel based on universally applied principles and tempered by a sense of balance in the distribution of blame cannot and should not be stigmatized as anti-Semitic, however mistaken or dangerous to Israel one might consider them to be. A good example can be found in the editorials published in the <u>New York Times</u> on Lebanon. Unlike the consistently superb editorials on Lebanon in the <u>Wall Street Journal</u>, the ones in the <u>Times</u> have been harsh on Israel, they have often been unfair, and they have pointed toward policies that would jeopardize Israel's security. But they have not been guided by the usual double standard, and therefore cannot and should not be stigmatized as anti-Semitic.

Criticisms of Israel that <u>are</u> informed by a double standard, on the other hand, deserve to be called anti-Semitic even when they are mouthed by Jews or, for that matter, Israelis. That being Jewish or possessing Israeli citizenship guarantees immunity from anti-Semitic ideas may seem a plausible proposition, but it is not, alas, borne out by experience. Like all other human beings, Jews are influenced by the currents of thought around them; and like all other minority groups, they often come to see themselves through the eyes of an unsympathetic or hostile majority. Jews are of course the majority in Israel, but the state itself is isolated among the nations, and subjected to a constant barrage of moral abuse aimed at its delegitimation. This seems finally to be taking the inevitable psychological toll in the appearance among Israelis of the term fascist in talking about their own society, when by any universal standard it is among the two or three countries in the world least deserving of this epithet.

To be sure, very few Israelis have reached the point of blaming the Arab-Israeli conflict largely on Israel or Menachem Begin or Ariel Sharon. But a number of American Jews have been adding their own special note to the whining chorus of anti-Israel columnists, State Department Arabists, and corporate sycophants of Saudi Arabia which has grown more raucous over Lebanon than ever before. The misleading impression has been created that these "dissenters" reveal a serious split within the American Jewish community over Israel. In fact, however, with a few notable exceptions they represent the same minority of roughly ten or fifteen percent which has all along either opposed Israel (because as socialists they considered Zionism a form of reactionary bourgeois nationalism or because as Reform Jews they disliked nationalism for other reasons), or else came to support Israel grudgingly and only on condition that it comport itself in accordance with their political ideas. It is these people who have lately been congratulating themselves on their courage in "speaking out" against Israel. A few of them -- those who live and work within the Jewish community -- are actually dissenting. But most of the rest live in milieux like the university or work in professions like journalism in which defending Israel takes far more courage than attacking it.

Not only do these people invoke a double standard in judging Israel: they proudly proclaim they do. "Yes, there is a double standard. From its birth Israel asked to be judged as a light among the nations." These words come from one of the endless series of columns Anthony Lewis has written on the war in Lebanon. Lewis is Jewish, and even though he makes no public point of it, I single him out here because his thinking is typical of the way Jewish "dissenters" who have been signing ads and giving interviews see not only the war in Lebanon but the Arab-Israeli conflict as a whole.

Thus while he usually pays his rhetorical respects to the Arab refusal to recognize Israel, Lewis's emphasis is always on the sins of Israel, whether real or imaginary.* And while piously proclaiming his great friendship for Israel, he harasses it relentlessly and obsessively, justifying himself in this by hiding behind the political opposition in Israel or behind Zionist heroes of the past like Brandeis. (Others use the Bible for these purposes, humbly comparing themselves to the prophets of old: "[The] biblical tradition of criticism and dissent should now guide public practice," two young Jewish academics declared on the Op-Ed page of the Times. "Jeremiah's polemics indicate that a government's foreign and security policies, as well as societal inequity and immorality, are grounds for legitimate dissent.")

But is it true that "From its birth Israel asked to be judged as a light among the nations," or even as the socialist paradise dreamed of by so many of Israel's Jewish "friends" on the Left? No doubt there have been Zionist enthusiasts who indulged in such rhetoric, but it is a historical travesty to claim that this was the animating idea behind the Jewish state. If perfection had been the requirement, it would have been tantamount to saying that an imperfect Israel had no right to exist; and since imperfection in human beings is unavoidable, Israel would have been sentencing itself to an early death from the day of its birth.

In any event, the opposite is more nearly true:

---

* For an example of the latter, see Ruth R. Wisse's discussion in "The Deligitimation of Israel," in the July Commentary. The case in point was a false allegation of censorship against the Israeli authorities on the West Bank, combined with complete silence about the repression of free speech on the East Bank -- that is, in Jordan.

that the purpose of Israel was to <u>normalize</u> the Jewish people, not to perfect them. The Jewish state was to create not a utopia but a refuge from persecution and a haven of security in which Jews who chose or were forced to settle there could live a peaceful and normal life. Thanks to the refusal of the Arab world to agree to this, the Jews of Israel have instead had to live in a constant state of siege. It would have been fully understandable if under those conditions Israel had become a garrison state or a military dictatorship. Yet no such development occurred. Founded as a democracy, it has remained a democracy, a particularly vital variant of the species -- the only one in the Middle East and one of the few on the face of the earth.

In reminding ourselves of that enormous and wondrous fact, we come to the greatest irony of this entire debate. Although Israel is no more required than any other state to justify its existence through what Anthony Lewis or anyone else, myself included, considers good behavior; and although elementary fairness dictates that Israel not be condemned for doing things that all other nations are permitted to do as a matter of course; even so, even judged by the higher standard that Lewis and his ilk demand, the truth is that Israel <u>has</u> become a light unto the nations.

Thus, in remaining a free democratic society while surrounded by enemies and forced to devote an enormous share of its resources to defense, Israel has demonstrated that external threats do not necessarily justify the repression of internal liberties. For casting this light, in whose glare the majority of the nations of the world stand exposed, Israel not surprisingly wins no friends at the UN.

If its persistence in democratic ways under the most unpromising circumstances has helped win Israel the enmity of the Third World, the fierceness of its will to live is what has made it a scandal and a reproach to its fellow democracies in the Western world. For in the glare of <u>that</u> light, the current political complexion of the Western democracies takes on a sickly, sallow, even decadent look. We in the West confront in the Soviet Union a deadly enemy sworn to our destruction, just as Israel does in the Arab world. But whereas the Israelis have faced the reality of their peril and have willingly borne the sacrifices essential to coping with it, we in the West have increasingly fallen into the habit of denial, and we have shown ourselves reluctant to do what the survival of our civilization requires. We tell ourselves that the danger comes from our own misunderstanding and misperception; we castigate ourselves for being the

main cause of the conflict; we urge unilateral action
upon ourselves in the hope of appeasing the enemy.

It is a rough rule of thumb that the more deeply
this complex of attitudes is rooted in an individual or
a group or a nation, the more hostility it will feel
toward Israel. I readily admit that other factors also
come into play. Anxiety over oil or business
connections in the Arab world often turn people against
Israel who might otherwise admire it precisely for
setting the kind of example of realism and courage they
would wish the West to follow. Secretary of Defense
Caspar Weinberger is perhaps one such case and there
are others scattered through the Defense Department,
the State Department, and the White House. There are
also so-called hard-liners where the Soviet Union is
concerned (Evans and Novak come to mind) who have
always believed that a tilt away from Israel and a more
"evenhanded" policy in the Middle East is necessary if
we are to contain the spread of Soviet power and
influence in that region. This idea dies so hard that
it may even survive the tremendous blow it has suffered
in Lebanon.

On the other side, one can find many American Jews
and liberal politicians concerned about Jewish support
who back Israel even though in most other situations
they tend to sympathize with forces comparable to the
PLO (such as the guerrillas in El Salvador) and even
though they are great believers in the idea that all
disputes can and should be settled through
negotiation.

Even allowing for these complications, however,
one can still say that the more committed to
appeasement of the Soviet Union a given party is, and
the more it opposes "military solutions to political
problems," the more hostile it will be to Israel. Thus
the West European governments -- the very governments
which are so eager to prop up the Soviet economy, to
ignore Afghanistan and Poland, and to ratify Soviet
military superiority in Europe through arms-control
negotiations -- are far less friendly to Israel than is
the American government. And within the United States
itself, the people who are most sympathetic to the
European point of view on the issue of the Soviet
threat are among those least friendly to Israel.

These are the same Americans who also tend to
pride themselves on having learned "the lessons of
Vietnam" -- lessons which, as Terry Krieger points out
in a brilliant piece in the Washington Times, Israel
has now dramatically refuted. For Israel has shown
that military force is sometimes necessary; that the
use of military force may also be beneficial; and that
a Soviet client, "whether it be a guerrilla force or a
terrorist organization," can be defeated by an American

ally. This, Krieger thinks, is why such people have
turned on Israel with vitriolic fury: "Those Americans
who have denounced Israel's invasion of Lebanon
eventually may forgive Israel for defending itself, but
they may never forgive Israel for illuminating our own
confusion and cowardice."

Again, Anthony Lewis offers himself as a good
illustration. Indeed, the terms in which he has
denounced Israel's invasion of Lebanon are strongly
reminiscent of the hysterical abuse he used to heap on
the United States in Vietnam. This being so, it is
worth remembering that Lewis called the Christmas 1972
bombing of Hanoi -- in which by the estimate of the
North Vietnamese themselves no more than 1,600 were
killed -- "The most terrible destruction in the history
of man" and a "crime against humanity." It is worth
recalling too that only days before the Khmer Rouge
Communists would stake a claim to precisely that
description by turning their own country into the
Auschwitz of Asia. Lewis greeted their imminent seizure
of power with the question: "What future possibility
could be more terrible than the reality of what is
happening to Cambodia now?" Yet with that record of
political sagacity and moral sensitivity behind him,
Lewis has the effrontery to instruct Israel on how to
insure its security, and he has the shamelessness to
pronounce moral judgment upon the things Israel does to
protect itself from the kind of fate at the hands of
the Arabs that has been visited by the Communists upon
South Vietnam and Cambodia.

The Bible tells us that God commanded the ancient
Israelites to "choose life," and it also suggests to us
that for a nation, the choice of life often involves
choosing the sacrifices and horrors of war. The people
of contemporary Israel are still guided by that
commandment and its accompanying demands. This is why
Israel is a light unto other peoples who have come to
believe that nothing is worth fighting or dying for.

But there is more. In the past, anti-Semitism has
been a barometer of the health of democratic societies,
rising in times of social or national despair, falling
in periods of self-confidence. It is the same today
with attitudes toward Israel. Hostility toward Israel
is a sure sign of failing faith in and support for the
virtues and values of Western civilization in general
and of America in particular. How else are we to
interpret a political position that, in a conflict
between a democracy and its anti-democratic enemies, is
so dead set against the democratic side?

Even on the narrower issue of American interests,
George Ball, Anthony Lewis, and those who share their
perspective are so driven by their animus against
Israel as to think that (in Lewis's astonishing words)

"Looking at the wreckage in Lebanon, the only people who can smile are the radicals and the Russians." Yet consider: Israel, an American ally, and armed with American weapons, has defeated the Syrians and the PLO, both of them tied to and armed by America's enemy, the Soviet Union. Are the Russians insane that this should cause them to smile? The military power of the PLO, representing the forces of radicalism and anti-Americanism in the Middle East, has been crushed; and (unless Ball and the others, who are so desperate to save it, should work their will) its power to terrorize and intimidate may also be destroyed, leaving the way open for such forces of moderation as may exist in the Arab world to come forward. How should this make the radicals smile and the United States weep? Egypt, America's best friend in the Arab world, has been strengthened and the policy of accommodation it has pursued toward Israel has been vindicated in comparison with the rejectionist policies of Syria and the PLO. Can this be good for the Russians and damaging to American interests?

George Ball says that it can be and that it is. But this is so palpably absurd that it cannot be taken as the considered judgment of an informed and objective mind. Therefore if it is proper to indict anyone in this debate for bias and insufficient concern for American interests, it is Ball who should be put in the dock and not the Jewish defenders of Israel against whom he himself has been pleased to file this very indictment.

In the broadside from which I have borrowed the title of this essay, Emile Zola charged that the persecutors of Dreyfus were using anti-Semitism as a screen for their reactionary political designs. I charge here that the anti-Semitic attacks on Israel which have erupted in recent weeks are also a cover. They are a cover for a loss of American nerve. They are a cover for acquiescence in terrorism. They are a cover for the appeasement of totalitarianism. And I accuse all those who have joined in these attacks not merely of anti-Semitism but of the broader sin of faithlessness to the interests of the United States and indeed to the values of Western civilization as a whole.

War Reporting: Path of Least Resistance
By Hodding Carter

...It is a commonplace to note television's apparently ungovernable appetite for the story with good footage, no matter how minor the incident, as opposed to major stories with inadequate or non-existent "visuals." That helps explain why more air time can be devoted to the wounding of a single demonstrator on the West Bank than to the equally factual but unfilmed slaughter of thousands of rebels in Syria.

But the problem goes deeper than television's mindless obeisance to its own technology and techniques. All but a handful of news organizations have cut back, rather than increased, the number of reporters stationed abroad. Getting the facts out on a war whose participants are not eager for coverage requires a lot of manpower and even more time. It risks, like good investigative journalism, coming up dry at the end of monumental labor.

Given the limited manpower available, the decision is repeatedly made to go where the sitting ducks are. This sometimes happens after a few ritual passes at breaking through the information curtain for the sake of journalistic conscience, but as often as not it occurs almost as soon as it becomes clear that a particular war will not be one which comes complete with briefing officers and taxpayer-paid trips to the front.

The payoff is that those most interested in suppressing the truth are given what amounts to a free ride while those who in fact believe that their people deserve at least some of the truth are penalized for being so open.

The tempting moral in this for the more open governments is that it would be wise to go back to the old rules. The best way for the press to counter that temptation is to try harder to get the really big stories -- such as the war between Iran and Iraq -- and to play the news according to the relative merit rather than according to relative ease in obtaining it, pictures and all.

War Coverage in a TV Age
By Nick Thimmesch

...The presence of TV cameras is a risk to the reputation of a combatant, but the price a free nation pays for that presence is worth it....

The loudest complaints about recent television coverage of military violence come from Israel and its supporters in the United States. Observers agree that since Israel was founded it enjoyed extraordinarily good treatment in the news and entertainment media, to the obvious disadvantage of the Arabs. In recent years, Arabs got better treatment, and the media turned away from showing Israel in romantic terms. Israel's high-technology military machine, superior to that of any Middle East nation, caused the media to cease portraying Israel as David vs. the Arab Goliath.

With all those TV crews in Beirut and Israel, it wasn't surpising that this invasion was seen on our TV screens for months. After all, an invasion is an invasion, and Israel's relentless bombing of Palestinian camps and Beirut neighborhoods, with the inevitable shots of wounded children and stunned elderly people staggering around -- well, that's TV footage.

True, only a fraction of similar mayhem was shown a few years back when PLO and leftist forces fought Phalangists in a quite violent civil war which took upwards of 60,000 lives. Nor was there much television footage of the casualties and destruction resulting from Israel's bombing attacks on Palestinian camps and of Beirut itself, in the period of years before last June's invasion.

Television cameras had access to this earlier violence, but news editors in New York expressed only occasional interest in coverage. During this 1975-1982 period, the PLO learned how to cultivate the media, so when Israel invaded, the cameras were ready. Israel's censorship of the invasion in its early stages only heightened the interest of TV correspondents to get the story.

But Israel's press and public is fiercely protective of its freedom, and these tactics backfired, particularly when the massacre story broke. People in a free society expect their media to show what their government and military are up to. The media can't be stifled.

The American media correctly react to their news instincts about the deportment of nations using the lethal power of American-supplied weapons....

We should televise more of the violence inflicted by nations and armies, not less. My hunch is that in a world loaded down with enormous quantities of conventional and highly sophisticated weapons -- many supplied by the United States -- television has been a force to reduce slaughter, and perhaps has given many poor souls a chance to live a few more precious years.

Reprinted by permission of <u>Public Opinion</u> from the October/November 1982 issue.

4
Discussion of Media Coverage in Central America

Daniel James, a veteran foreign correspondent, long experienced in writing from and about Latin America, introduced the discussion of how the troubles in Central America are being reported. He began with some remarks about his own recent investigations for a book on media coverage of the area.

DANIEL JAMES: I've read and researched more than three thousand stories, news analyses, news features, editorials and Op-Ed pieces that have been published or broadcast in what might be called, for want of a better term, the "prestige media." Admittedly arbitrary, the term as I use it in my book, embraces the New York Times, the Washington Post, Time and Newsweek magazines, and the ABC, CBS and NBC television networks. The period covered was from October 15, 1979, when Salvadoran Army junior officers overthrew a dictatorship, to October 15, 1982. I have also done a large amount of reading and research of other materials not disseminated by the prestige media, including books, pamphlets and other literature, representing various points of view, in both Spanish and English; they proved to be most valuable for background purposes as well as contemporary insights. And of course, as has already been said, I have been covering the area for a long time -- thirty-one years -- lived there during most of the period, and have read widely in Spanish.

My examination of prestige media coverage of El Salvador leads to the conclusion that they are guilty of many errors of both commission and omission. Much the same is true, futher research indicates, of their coverage also of Nicaragua during the same period. Since my point of view, naturally, is that of a journalist, what struck me perhaps more than anything else was that their coverage departed considerably from the traditional principles of journalism -- which is to say, of objectivity and fairness -- and too often suffered from a lack of accuracy and of hard information.

Research indicates, also, that a number of prestige media reporters either went into El Salvador with an emotional, political or ideological bias, or developed one while they were there. This bias usually was reflected in the form of sympathy or at least a "positive" attitude toward the guerillas, and on the other hand an antipathy, or a "negative" attitude toward the Salvadoran government and its armed forces. Most of the time the guerillas were not identified as "Marxist" or "Marxist-led," about which there is no doubt, leaving the public with only a vague notion of who or what they represented. I'm sorry that Ray Bonner isn't here, because he is typical of what I mean. As he once told a discussion group organized by the Center for the Study of Democratic Institutions, held on the West Coast, he was reluctant to apply the adjective "Marxist" or "Marxist-led" to the guerillas because he felt that would be "negative." I agree that the Marxist image is a negative one, but clearly it is the duty of a Western journalist to report it.

I should like to offer, quickly, to support two import conclusions I reached as a result of my study, and then we can get on to the discussion. The first, as I have mentioned, is that much of the prestige media's coverage of Central America has been very biased, leading one to conclude that it comes under the heading of tendentious or advocacy journalism. The second is that often the material presented in the print and electronic media is based upon partisan or discredited sources of information, which are therefore unreliable.

Let me be specific. For a long time, stories were dispatched from El Salvador reporting on human rights violations that were based upon information provided, chiefly, by the Legal Aid Office and the Human Rights Commission, which were purported to be speaking for the Salvadoran Catholic Church. In that way, they were invested with the aura of ecclesiastical authority. But the prestige media ignored -- and to this day have continued to ignore -- the fact that the Salvadoran Church had repudiated those sources of information publicly, officially, on at least three separate occasions. It actually charged those sources with being "partisan" and even with "sowing confusion." Yet the Church's disavowal of them was not carried in the prestige media, with the sole exception of an item by Christopher Dickey in the Washington Post, while they continued to rely upon the same sources. That is one major example of the media's use of partisan and discredited sources of information on El Salvador.

The more than three thousand pieces I researched

also turned up too many examples of stories based on few, or even no facts, to substantiate the conclusions or opinions their writers reached. I shall cite, for example, a story by a <u>Washington Post</u> correspondent, Alma Guillermoprieto, that the paper published in November 1981. Her lead was that the Salvadoran government had virtually lost the war to the guerillas, who had taken over one-quarter of the country and were about to overrun it altogether. There was not a single fact in her lead, not even a quotation from somebody to substantiate it. About three paragraphs down she confessed that it was based on "assessments," made by diplomats, rebel leaders, military people, and so on. One reads on hoping to find the names of those persons, but in vain. For something like 128 column inches, beginning on page one and going through two jumps, Guillermoprieto fails to identify a single diplmomat, rebel leader, or anyone else who had made any "assessments" that might bolster her lead and its conclusion that the Marxists were winning the war in El Salvador.

She did quote one person in her story, but he was not a diplomat, rebel leader or military observer, and he is here today, Bob Leiken. What Alma Guillermoprieto quoted was not something first-hand, either, but testimony Bob had given to a House subcommittee two months before the article appeared. That is all. Now, fine, if you want to write an editorial saying the rebels are winning, that's the writer's prerogative. But the <u>Post</u> was passing this off as a news report from El Salvador.

Sources are rarely checked against each other. One example comes from the writings of our friend Ray Bonner of the <u>New York Times</u>. A story of his, since become famous, concerns torture classes allegedly given by Salvadoran soldiers and witnessed by U.S. military advisers. Bonner didn't bother to check out his only source, a Salvadoran Army deserter named Carlos Gomez Montano. Although the <u>New York Times</u> said that Bonner had gone to people to check out Gomez's account, the fact is that its publisher, Arthur Hays Sulzberger, felt impelled after the story's appearance to write a letter acknowledging that the story was a "mistake", it had been "overplayed" -- to use his words -- and was based on the unverified information of a single individual. Nevertheless, that misleading story, which in effect slandered Americans in uniform, was prominently displayed in the <u>Times</u> without being checked.

Another criticism my study leads me to make is that the average U.S. journalist who has gone into El Salvador has been largely ignorant of its history, its culture, and most certainly its language. How anybody can get around in any Spanish-speaking country without knowing Spanish, particularly in rural El Salvador, where even persons fluent in the tongue have a problem communicating with the average person, is beyond me.

I have also found that there is a distinct overplaying on this issue of human rights. I know I'm treading on very delicate ground. I share with everyone at this table a concern over the brutality, the unheard-of brutality, of the Salvadoran armed forces and particularly the so-called death squads. Nobody in his or her right mind can condone what they have done and continue to do. By all means, let's continue to expose human rights violations, but let us not do so at the expense of overlooking or distorting other issues that are also important.

There are other issues. The overriding one is whether freedom or dictatorship will rule El Salvador. By "dictatorship" I mean, specifically, totalitarian dictatorship, which would close the door to all freedoms for the people of El Salvador. That would result in violating the rights of the entire nation, incarcerating it in a gulag. Let us not ignore that danger in our zeal to protect individual rights.

In a similar vein, I found in my study that the prestige media have been guilty of alarmism, in raising the specter of "another Vietnam" occurring in El Salvador. Researching for a chapter on the subject, I found that the prestige media supplied no serious evidence that such a phenomenon was likely to happen.

But the result of media alarmism on the subject has been to create a feeling approaching panic in this country -- that perhaps we are going to become involved in another situation like Vietnam. Yet there are no grounds in Salvadoran reality for such a supposition. (A footnote: I hear no voices of alarm raised about stationing some 1200 Marines in Lebanon, where the situation is far more explosive than the one in El Salvador. In Lebanon, they really are in a state of advanced warfare; mines are all over the place, major combat is going on continuously, the capital is bombed regularly until it has become a shambles. Yet we do not see the media becoming alarmist over the alleged danger of another "Vietnam" there.)

Of course, bitter memories of Vietnam have inhibited the conduct of U.S. foreign policy in El Salvador, understandably. And I am not justifying the Reagan administration's policies in that country when I say that. Nor do I excuse the hysteria aroused by Al Haig as Secretary of State, when the high level of rhetoric from the beginning of the administration contributed to the media's perception of the problem of El Salvador.

But back to the media's performance. They have

found themselves involved not only in disseminating guerilla propaganda but also in lending credence to downright forgery used for propaganda purposes, which they accepted trustingly. I refer specifically to the "dissent paper" which began circulating around Washington within forty-eight hours after Reagan's election in 1980. Anthony Lewis was gullible enough to fall for it, in his New York Times column, but it was Flora Lewis who played it up in her column for the same paper, early in March 1981. She wrote that the "dissent paper" had been drafted by persons from various government agencies, the State Department in particular, who disagreed with President Carter's policies in El Salvador and wanted to influence his successor to change them. Well, it turned out that no such document ever existed in reality; it was a forgery. Flora Lewis -- thank God she had the courage to acknowledge this -- admitted in a follow-up column that it was "spurious," and that "I was duped."

There are other cases where media persons reporting on Central America may have been duped by leftist guerilla propaganda, misinformation, whatever you want to call it. Plenty of examples are available.

Happily, the media have shown a capacity for self-criticism. In the case of El Salvador, and to some extent Nicaragua, a fair number of pieces have appeared, notably in the Washington Post, that criticized their own performance in the former country. I think this is a very healthy trend and I hope it continues. Also, there has been effective criticism outside the media, of their shortcomings, particularly of the leaning of some of them toward advocacy and tendentiousness.

Let journalists write or broadcast what they please. I say that's fine. But don't pass off as "news" what should be clearly labeled as opinion or editorial matter. And don't call "news analysis" that which usually contains little or no news and is basically "analysis," that is, opinion. Such subterfuges only delude the public, deprive it of its right to know. The public clearly has the right to receive true information: information unvarnished by the biases or prejudices or partisan interests of the one reporting it, to the extent that that is humanly possible. That, I think, is the fundamental issue to be faced in discussing media coverage of Central America.

CHAIRMAN: I asked Dan James to summarize his ideas, drawing upon the research he has been doing on media coverage of Central America. This he has done with candor and conviction. He has given us a provocative beginning. I had intended to have Ray Bonner come next. But Bonner, who as late as yesterday was hoping to be here, warned me that the assignment he was working on for the _Times_ might keep him away. And, indeed, unfortunately, he was not able to come. I am sure he would have some interesting points to make if he were here. Now, let us simply throw the meeting open for comments from anybody who wants to speak.

ALLEN WEINSTEIN: I don't intend to speak for Ray Bonner but I did spend some time, not very much time, in El Salvador and Nicaragua earlier this year in a delegation that included many journalists. Despite the very diverse background of the people in our group we issued a unanimous report condemning violations of press freedom -- which we certainly found in both countries.

I would like to begin by taking issue with some of Dan James's premises -- from a position that is somewhat safe in the sense that I edit a little quarterly which is not part of the prestige media. Let's look at that term. The term as I understand it has come into existence and is used in the pejorative sense. It is not a descriptive term. My feeling is that it is not helpful. In the analyses of the "prestige media" we generally overlook the regional papers which have such profound influence on public opinion in their own sections of the country -- the _Chicago Tribune_, the _Los Angeles Times_, the _Miami Herald_ (especially the _Miami Herald_ which is so active in covering Latin America). Why are they not part of the prestige media? In my definition, I would include them, but normally they are not absorbed into this analysis because, in part, they use so much wire-service copy. But they do a damn good job of balancing off opinions with analyses and straight news and information.

Is MacNeil/Lehrer, of PBS, considered part of the prestige media? Normally, it is omitted, by definition. But this is the one single news program that does more to shape the opinions among opinion-holders in this country than any other. I don't know what the three thousand articles are that you have been analysing. I really look forward to reading your book because I respect your work.

I'm not sure that some of these problems aren't endemic to journalism. When the hell was Latin American coverage ever excellent? I think that it is probably better today in terms of what we get from the people going down there now than it ever has been. The history of our hit-or-miss coverage of Latin America goes back to the nineteenth century. We have had American journalists wandering in and out of Latin

America covering wars and revolutions, changes in political machines and so on, with neither rhyme nor reason, normally without background, without speaking the language, normally drifting in and drifting out in a haphazard fashion. That is the way it has been for many years, a process that has continued until very recently.

Karen [DeYoung], you can correct me on this, do all of the major papers now maintain full-scale bureaus in various parts of Latin America? Or do they tend to work out of Mexico City and Miami?

So among other things, we don't even have the constant coverage that does get around the whole area for the very simple reason that Latin America is considered by the U.S. press as a kind of backwater region. It is important to look at revolutions, it is important what regimes that we don't like may be coming into existence. But, by and large, the area has not received the systematic, sustained political attention that it deserves. With the exception of some of the coverage, particularly in the Post, one would be hard-pressed -- talking about the major mass media -- to identify the key political groupings in countries like Nicaragua or El Salvador, if you were just a casual reader of our papers, because the focus often tends to be on the military aspects of the war.

However, I'm not at all certain that journalists are somehow less qualified today than was once the case. My guess is that if you looked at this over a period of time you'd find more of them speaking Spanish, more of them having done graduate work on Latin American affairs than ever before. I have to say to Dan James: Of the sins that you were describing, insofar as they were sins, I'm not sure I agree with your description. The complaints you are making seem to me to be less about qualifications than about conclusions. Here is where I think events like our discussion today serve a useful purpose. I'm not sure what Ray Bonner thinks about the best outcome of the war in El Salvador but I think I can make a reasonable guess based on reading his articles. And I'm not certain that I object to Ray Bonner or anyone else with those views covering the war if they can distinguish clearly between news coverage and news analysis. They have a right to their assessment as every journalist does. This is a problem as much for editors as for journalists and I think, thanks in part to the controversy surrounding this issue, we are getting better editing all through the prestige media on these matters. Opinion pieces are being labeled clearly as opinion pieces more than was the case a few years ago.

I'm not certain the way to encourage better coverage in Central America, or any place, is to send a group of journalists who are sworn not to have political opinions on anything or not to inject their political opinions into their coverage. I think what we're looking for is a greater pluralism of coverage so that you can, in the major media at least, have a wider range of perspectives on even matters of analysis. But I fret over the dangers of getting too much of the scatter-gun effect here because the basic argument that coverage has been profoundly biased and unbalanced in Central America. I just don't believe that is the case. One can make an argument about picking and choosing articles about any part of the world from the right or the left or from any political perspective; it's a question of selection. What I fear is that the argument could degenerate into an eventual accusation that the media "lost" Central America.

WILLIAM LEOGRANDE: I'm not a journalist and have no pretensions of being one, so I won't engage some of the very important issues that are at stake for professional journalists in how you go about covering this type of conflict. I do want to say, at the risk of being a bit provocative, and with all respect to Mr. James, that I think he's mistaken right down the line on most of the points that he's made. It does not seem to me that the coverage of Central America has been biased and tendentious. The press has certainly identified the guerillas as Marxist-led and has gone into great detail about the political background and political attitudes of the armed groups as well as the non-armed groups, the Social Democratic and Christian Democratic elements. And certainly the press has reported at great length on the position of the United States government with regard to these groups, printing the text of such things as the State Department white paper. The New York Times printed the text of that white paper three times: once when it was leaked, once when it was presented on the Hill, and the final version when it was publicly released -- the same document three times. The Miami Herald printed the text of the document prepared by the State Department on the political backgrounds of the guerilla leaders of the FMLN. The Times printed the documents on Cuban-Soviet military relations and their connection to Central America.

It seems to me that the reporting has been pretty reasonable in that regard; the opposition in Salvador could make a good case that the government of the United States and the government of El Salvador have much better access to the prestige press in the United States than they do.

With regard to bias and discredited sources such as the Salvadoran human rights organizations, the relationship of various human rights organizations to the Church and particularly the Archbishop's office is a very complicated issue. When it became clear that this was an important issue and a complex one, the press did a good job of reporting those complexities. I remember a story in the <u>Post</u> that went to great lengths to specify the reporting methodologies and the political connections of each of the Salvadoran human rights organizations and where they got their data.

With regard to stories with "few facts," that is an issue of how far you go with a story that's based on unattributed sources. That is an important issue that journalists themselves have to come to terms with. I'll just recall an article in <u>Newsweek</u> magazine, the cover story about the secret war in Nicaragua; it did not have, to my recollection, a single attributed quote anywhere in it. Some of these kinds of stories can't be done with clear attribution because people won't go on record. I don't think that means you ignore a story, but there is an important issue on how you play such a story.

With regard to sources not being checked and particularly the example of the Ray Bonner story on torture, I'd be interested in some other examples. Every time this issue comes up, that is the story the public affairs officer at the embassy in El Salvador points to as evidence that Ray Bonner did not know what he was doing. It seems to me that story was as much the fault of the editor as it was of Ray Bonner. Bonner got the story, and sent it to New York. I understand it was held for a while to see if it couldn't be confirmed. Isn't it then the editor's decision whether to go with that single-source story or not?

Do the reporters know a lot about Salvadoran history and culture? I was in El Salvador a few weeks ago and, being an academic, I expect journalists not to really know much background about a country. I expect them to be focusing on the breaking news and not really able to bring to it much historical analysis or analytic understanding. But I must say that, having spent a good amount of time in conversation with reporters in El Salvador, I was extremely impressed by them. I was impressed with their level of historic understanding, I was surprised and impressed by the sophistication and complexity of the analysis that they brought to events -- even journalists who had only been there for a short time.

Whether the human rights issue has been overplayed, I think is a knotty problem. It's not the business of the press to predict what the outcome of the war will be, totalitarianism or whatever, but it is their job to report what is happening now. If that includes reporting on human rights violations by the government of El Salvador then so be it. I don't think the press ought to be in the business of saying that the human rights issue is overplayed in the United States and that's why the American people are unwilling to support the government of El Salvador. That should be an op-ed piece.

Is El Salvador being reported as "another Vietnam?" I don't think the press has indulged in sensationalism about another Vietnam. There is a real reaction of people in the Congress and the American public to the danger of another Vietnam. The press has simply reported on that reaction. To denounce the media for this matter is really a case of cutting off the head of the messenger who brings the bad news.

As to the "dissent paper" which you called a forgery and propaganda by which the media was duped, my sense is that the press handled that issue very well. No one knew where the dissent paper came from when it turned up on people's desks back in November of 1980. For two or three months, the press paid no attention to it at all precisely because they couldn't figure out where it came from. Efforts to find out proved to no avail. Two columnists, Anthony Lewis and Flora Lewis, did columns on it. Anthony Lewis apparently understood the strange nature of the document and was very careful in the way he presented it; he really talked about the arguments that were made in it rather than whether it was an official document or not. Flora Lewis made the mistake of thinking that it was an official dissent channel document which it was not. She acknowledged her error, as you pointed out. However, we still don't know where that document came from and frankly, in my efforts to find out, I was told by several people in the Reagan administration that the content of the document suggested people in the administration had been involved in putting it together. So I don't think you can call it guerilla propaganda and I think that, in fact, the press handled it in a very responsible way.

Finally, this whole controversy over press coverage in El Salvador really began in early 1981 when a few reporters had the opportunity, for the first time, to go into the guerilla controlled zones in El Salvador and report on what they saw. That raised the issue of how journalists should deal with controlled tours. I think that that is an important issue for journalists to grapple with. But my sense in reading those stories was that most of the journalists who went on the tours were very careful to specify what they were told and what they were shown was from the guerilla point of view. In reading their stories, one did not get the sense that these reporters had been taken in, but rather that they were reporting what they saw and the conditions under which they saw them. I think it was the content of what they saw that galvanized a certain pressure on the press, criticism that it was portraying the guerillas in too favorable a light. The Wall Street Journal editorial became the famous shot across the bow in that regard. In substantive terms, however, those articles turn out to be very good articles.

The chairman then called on Karen DeYoung, of the Washington Post, who had reported extensively from Central America and whose coverage at times had been under discussion.

KAREN DEYOUNG: I would just like to say that Bill LeoGrande said pretty much what I would say. But let me start off with a word about the resources of the Post in Central America. We now have three bureaus covering the region. The members of these bureaus all speak Spanish. I think they all operate quite well in rural El Salvador. They are all experienced journalists. When I started working in Latin America in 1976 we had one bureau in all of Latin America and that was in Argentina to cover Centeral America, Mexico, and all of South America. It was not a high priority bureau.
    Going down through the points that Dan James has raised, I think that you picked out some examples that all of us have heard and discussed a number of times. I think they are both selectively chosen and perhaps a little bit misrepresented. One important story you mentioned was the one by Alma Guillermoprieto about the lack of military control over certain parts of the country. That story, which I remember quite well, came from the U.S. Embassy and the U.S. military group and was discussed with then-Colonel Garcia who happened to be here in Washington at the time. Like many such stories, the information and the assessments that were presented in that story were given to us on the basis that they not be attributed to any person by name. We have, with certain caveats, an obligation to cover, to present those kinds of assessments just as we have an obligation to cover regular briefings, background briefings that are held at the State Department even though we are not allowed to say who is doing the talking. Secretary Enders and other people do this sort of thing quite regularly.
    Again I would agree with Bill -- the same thing I would say on one of the other points; our job is not to project what we think the outcome of a struggle, such as the struggle in El Salvador, will be. I think our obligation is to explain who the people are who are fighting, what their backgrounds are, what they say and

what they do. Anything beyond that is the subject of editorial opinion.

Whether press coverage has inhibited the conduct of U.S. policy -- I find that a somewhat strange observation. I think the role of the press is to enhance the quality of U.S. policy by informing people of what is going on. If an administration, this administration or any before it, perceives that as an inhibition then I think that is a separate topic for discussion about the role of the press in general in this country.

The so-called dissent paper -- I don't know if I'd call it a forgery; the title page purported it to be something that no one was ever able to prove that it was. In fact, the first time that the dissent paper was mentioned in the Washington Post was in a series of articles that I did in February 1981, in which I said that the document's authenticity as an official document had been repudiated by both the Carter and Reagan administrations, that no one knew where it came from but that Carter administration people at the time felt that the information in it was essentially correct in terms of the characterization of policy. The same Freedom House report cited earlier somewhat misinterpreted the issue because it used the dissent paper as an example of how the press had been duped and how it had misreported these things. It stated that I said it was a real document when in fact I never said that.

One can look at different kinds of propaganda that have been disseminated. I think there was some question raised about the documents that were attached to the white paper issued officially by the administration. Criticism of what has been written about that white paper has been somewhat skewed. Articles in both the Washington Post and the Wall Street Journal, in fact, did not talk about the accuracy of the information or the independent accuracy of the conclusions of the white paper itself. What they talked about was a statement in the paper that the conclusions themselves were supported by the documents presented. Well, in the view of the people who wrote those stories, those conclusions were not supported by the document. There were other conclusions that were supported by those documents. We didn't feel it was a question of whether we thought the documents themselves were real or not but just how the whole package was presented. And yet, I think this issue has gotten so polarized and so tendentious, as you said, that criticism very often doesn't relate to reality.

DAVID NEWSOM: Could I throw one question on the table which you might also want to address? It has frequently been said that when you're dealing with a situation like El Salvador, where there is a war going on, the military action obscures the economic and social trends and the politics of the country. To some degree, therefore, coverage of the fighting obscures the basic issues that are at stake, and this is particularly true for television. I wonder, Dan James, if your analysis of the three thousand articles touched at all on that question: the war and the fighting action versus the basic issues involved.

DANIEL JAMES: Yes, a lot has been written about that, of course. Again, I refer to those who critique the media coverage as a search for what was called "bang-bang" in all kinds of crazy situations. Principally we are talking about TV in which the broadcast media resort to gimmicks in order to get some exciting shots which they can put on the evening news.

On the question of sensationalism in the print media, I have brought with me the opening paragraph of a story which says "the Salvadoran army appears to have lost control of approximately one-fourth of El Salvador's territory to guerilla forces and is in imminent danger of losing land access to nearly half the country if the rebels continue a spectacular bridge demolition campaign." Now that story was published November 10, 1981, a matter of mere months after the defeat of the guerillas in their "final offensive" of January of the same year. So how they could have accumulated all that strength as to threaten to take over the whole country is beyond me.

KAREN DEYOUNG: If I may just respond briefly to that. I don't think that the government of El Salvador has ever disputed that the FMLN controlled large portions, if not all, of three, or three-and-a-half provinces in the country. The policy of the government at that time, and still to some extent, was not to take over those provinces and basically to concentrate their efforts on avoiding economic targets. I don't think they disputed the blowing up of the bridges.

JAMES LOBE: Let me add to that. On October 21, 1981, there was a rather sensational column by Evans and Novak that quoted U.S. government sources accusing the Cubans of having blown up a bridge across the Rio Lempa and asserted the presence of Cubans in El Salvador. In that light they also raised the question of whether the entire eastern third of the country would then become an FMLN preserve. It was a very hot question among all kinds of journalists, not just those you label advocacy journalists from the opposite advocation at the time. They too were quoting government sources here and

Pentagon sources. I don't think it was as off-the-wall as Dan James suggests.

MARGARET HAYES: I'm not sure if it is worth saying anything from my perspective as a consumer of the media; in my case, limited entirely to print media. I was struck by a discussion, which, Karen, you participated in some time ago, in which the head of the New York Times bureau remarked: "Gee, I wonder how influential our coverage was on the Senate decision on land reform: statements were made by the committee on the reduction of funding and our authorization at the time." I was impressed by what I regarded as the extreme naivete of that statement because the coverage in the Washington Post and the New York Times is bound to be influential with the Congress. That, inevitably, places heavy responsibility on the major media, particularly because that is what is read, mostly at 7:00 in the morning when people get up here in Washington, to help them to decide what the truth or lack of truth is about what is going on in El Salvador.
     While it may be fine to say that there are reporters who know the situation better in Latin America -- and that is undoubtedly the case -- most of the people who read the press and are required to react on the spot are very little informed about the situation in that country. Particularly, they are very little informed about the differences between what El Salvador and Nicaragua and any other country looks like. There is a great lack of understanding of the different cultural and political and social background against which all these events play. I think that this has been, from my perspective, the area in which we have the greatest lack of information, particularly in the case of El Salvador.
     We see pictures of a lot of specific events on the war; we have very little understanding of how the country is trying itself to resolve its problems. There is an awful lot of commentary, pro and con, on U.S. policy; and I would always be careful about which government source I quoted. There is very little understanding here of the dynamics of the steps being taken by the oppostion or the government to accomplish their goals.
     In the aftermath of the elections in El Salvador there was a change in the type or volume of coverage -- and of reaction to it. Here again is my argument on responsibility of the media, for the kind of coverage that was printed in the Post and the Times did color the reactions of people in the policy and decision-making community. Given the very long learning curve that these people go through, it's six months before the weight of opinion is able to shift to

a different understanding of the situation. This points to this question of responsibility, but I'm not sure how one judges whether coverage is responsible or not. I'll just leave with people in the media my concern about the impact that coverage has on the policy-making community in Washington.

ROBERT LEIKEN: I'll make my remark very brief because I have to run back to my office and prepare testimony on El Salvador for Monday's hearing.

I wanted to pick up on what Margaret was talking about, what she said about elections in light of your remark on television. I think that the pictures on the TV screen, on the Sunday of elections in El Salvador, of long lines of voters, had an impact on the American public, on the American press and on the Congress that was tremendous. At the same time, I think it was unfortunate in the sense that it portrayed the election in a way that proved to be inaccurate.

I think this was also true of the press coverage. It raised a question in my mind, even from the week before elections, as to whether the reporters felt a certain pressure to corroborate or at least to devote very much attention to the administration's point of view as a result of criticism that had been made of their earlier coverage. And, let me say, some of that criticism I share. But I think that the result of the election coverage per se was that the American public and American policy makers were reinforced in their false impressions of El Salvador. Tom Brokaw's report covering the Salvadoran elections from "election central in San Salvador," as if returns were coming in from Iowa, turned out, I think, to be very misleading. It would be very interesting to explore why that shift in style of coverage did occur and what kinds of pressure were felt and where that pressure was coming from.

I would just like to mention two other areas where the press, I think, does need to try harder, even though I share a basic appreciation for its work in El Salvador. I think in Honduras the situation is very disturbing in terms of a drift toward what could eventually be a very unbalanced situation. It is U.S. policy to defend and help preserve democracy in Central America, but if Honduras becomes something like a Somoza-type regime, then we are going to have to ask what it is we're defending in Central America.

The other area that needs more careful media work is Nicaragua where it is very difficult for the press to function and to find out what is going on inside the Sandinista regime, how much Soviet and Cuban influence exists, or even what violations of human rights have occurred. That's a very difficult issue: the question of covering Nicaragua where it is very difficult for the press to function and to find out what is going on inside the Sandinista regime, how much Soviet and Cuban influence exists, or even what violations of human rights have occurred. That's a very difficult issue: the question of covering Nicaragua.

PAT ELLIS: I would like to address the question raised about TV coverage. I think one important thing has to be borne in mind. There have been pictures of wars and there always will be crises and disasters to cover. At the same time, I think we have seen an increase in the attempts on the part of certain segments of the media, both in the commercial networks and on public television -- MacNeil/Lehrer, Nightline, and other programs -- to do serious analysis of the issues. And you must bear in mind that in all these issues a very important part of the story is Washington and must be covered from Washington. It cannot be covered only from the field. The dilemmas facing Congress, and the administration and the American public -- these are things that are debated here and should be. What is happening there, on the ground, is part of the story, of course, but you have to take the Washington angle into account in your evaluation of how the media is covering things.

I would like to say that I think it would be great if we had more documentaries. I know documentaries have a very low priority on American television. Public television hasn't had the money of commercial television; and neither has viewed documentaries as a very high priority. I recall a conspicuous example of this indifference to serious documentaries: one on South Africa done by Bill Moyers which was aired at 10:00 p.m. on the Monday of Labor Day weekend.

These things being said, I think there are people in the broadcast media who care. There are people who are trying to get the information out, but it is a continual struggle. I am constantly trying to get people on our program, but sometimes it is easier for the print media to get people to talk off the record. I could give numerous examples of the difficulty in getting people to talk on television. The first time we had Assistant Secretary Thomas Enders on our program was just after the recent certification issue came to the fore. I had been trying for over a year to get him on. For so long we could get no one from the administration to come and represent their point of view. Now, we certainly do try and I think that is a very important point to bear in mind.

I have tried on numerous occasions to get the ambassador from El Salvador to come on our program, but it just seems that it is very difficult for me to come up with somebody who is acceptable for him to appear with. We have problems from all sides; it is not that we don't try. Let's look at the positive things that are being done and not exaggerate the other aspects of the coverage. Let's give credit to those professional journalists who are trying to do a good job.

Since so many Americans are getting their news from television, I think that those who care should be thinking a lot about how television coverage should be improved. That is not to say we should disregard the need to improve the coverage in print. Each branch of the media has its own problems in coverage, but we are dealing with different factors. We should be thinking about how we might treat these problems instead of focusing on criticism of what one particular journalist has done.

JEFF BIGGS: This question is contentious enough without my trying to make contentious points. I think my main concern is more with the mechanics of the process of covering a story like this than it is anything else. In that sense, I think it is obviously a shared responsibility between journalism and government. There are limitations on both sides that circumscribe the ways and the degree to which the average member of the public gets a full picture. I can start out by saying that I think MacNeil/Lehrer is one of the best reporting, not only visual, media vehicles around.

On the other hand, I am conscious of the fact that we turn down on a regular basis innumerable requests for on-the-record interviews. The fact is that it is not simply a matter of when the media feels it is an appropriate time to make a comment, it is also a matter of when the government feels it is. Most journalists recognize that, and there is a certain amount of disgruntlement on both sides. There are times when the government has to address an issue, like it or not. There are times when it would like to address an issue but when, in fact, the media is not particularly concerned.

The State Department noon briefing is probably a classic case in point. That is the chief vehicle by which the State Department makes an on-the-record statement as to what policy is on any given issue. But it also has a responsive function. I grant there is an announcement aspect of the noon briefing which allows the department to make a prepared statement but, also, you've got the spokesman up there with a great big black book of "guidances" who says something on most issues only in response to questions. That means that there are days that go one after another when there is a good statement to make or a policy to clarify which never gets on the record because nobody asks the question. That's a function of the way the system works rather than anything else.

Another issue is the way Central America is covered. If former Secretary of State Haig had never said "Let's go to the source," or if the guerillas' January offensive had never taken place as it did, or if the analysis had not been virtually instantaneous, I wonder, frankly, to what degree Central America would have received the kind of coverage it did receive. You can lament it. It's simply a fact that such statements and happenings focussed attention on Central America for the public, for the government, and for the media, that it had not received for a long time -- if ever. You get into the question of who sets the foreign policy agenda. Traditionally, one would argue that the administration sets the foreign policy agenda. I'm not sure that really is as true any longer. You can make as good a case that, to a large extent, Congress sets an agenda. You can make a case that the public, to a small degree, does vis-à-vis special interests. I'm not saying it's good or bad, but the fact is that several key actors influence the coverage and the policy agenda.

Now, we all know, you can go through weeks or months when there is very little Central American coverage. That imposes, it seems to me, both on the journalist and on the government, the necessity to fill in the gaps that precede the next high point in media coverage. This is a shared burden but I think it's a burden that's got to be accepted because things have been taking place; noteworthy things in terms of policy and news coverage. Filling in the gaps is less a problem for the print media than for the visual media. Battles are visually dramatic. Election lines are visually dramatic. But background negotiations among rival political parties is pretty tough to cover photographically, with any sense of drama. As a result, they don't get covered. I think we have to admit that television has a greater impact on the public's perception of what is going on in Central America than the New York Times, the Washington Post, the Wall Street Journal, the Christian Science Monitor, or the Chicago Tribune alone, or maybe even combined. Serious analysis, any sort of in-depth coverage, can basically be found largely in the print media. There are few bureaus established for regular, steady television coverage in Central America. So, it's generally a matter of getting together a crew, sending them down for ten days, doing the coverage and getting back. That's a pretty spotty way to cover something if, in fact, one has concluded it is worth some sort of sustained coverage.

Another example. There was a period of time when

there was a visible dichotomy between editorial
commentary on Central America and news commentary. You
could, in the same newspaper, read a news story written
from one point of view -- I don't mean a biased point
of view, but reflecting a definite point of view -- and
an editorial with a point of view 180 degrees in the
other direction. It gets even more complicated if you
look at another reality: that Central America has to be
covered in part from the on-the-ground viewpoint and
also from the Washington viewpoint. It's even more
complicated when you have on one newspaper a journalist
covering Congressional hearings, not a Central America
expert, who does not regularly cover Central America
but covers the Hill, and another staffer, a White House
correspondent who covers the White House, also not a
Central America expert, but, on this day, the President
or somebody else has something to say on Central
America. Still other reporters for the same paper may
be covering the same story from the State Department
and from the Pentagon. You get a variety, sometimes a
confusion, of viewpoints, and perhaps none of them
brings any substantive Central American background to
bear on what is the news of that day.

I get calls every day on: "What is the military
assistance level for El Salvador this year?" These are
available facts. Now maybe it is the responsibility of
the government to make sure everybody has them.
Perhaps we are not getting the raw data out; I'm not
talking about analysis or point of view. But these are
the facts which are ascertainable and yet I've seen the
level of military assistance written up at about
fifteen different levels. Some papers have covered it
accurately, some have not. I think, in part, that is
because news coverage on this issue is divided up among
a lot of different people, none of whom can cover it on
a sustained basis.

LANDRUM BOLLING: What about the problems of the editor
back home on the desk? It has been said that news is
often what the editor says it is. How do you deal with
the uncertainty or the sheer lack of knowledge and
understanding on the part of the editors on the desk as
to what is a story and how to play it?

JEFF BIGGS: I can remember vividly the day that I
stopped getting calls just from the eastern
establishment newspapers or media and began getting
calls from places like Boise, Idaho, from editorial
page editors who said, "Look, we've been treating this
story based upon either the New York Times or the
Washington Post news services or the wire services and
we finally decided that we want to look at this
ourselves, so, can you take me back to 1979 and bring

me up to the present?" That's when we stopped dealing in thirty second responses and started getting involved in twenty to twenty-five minute long distance phone calls. I think that's good. Despite the respect I have for the eastern establishment press, I would frankly far prefer to see the editors in Boise, Idaho, doing this from their own perspective rather than thinking their treatment all had to come from half a dozen major media sources. But it's difficult. The Washington Post is a superb newspaper, if you can read between the lines. But, if you live in Laramie, Wyoming, and can't read between the lines, it's difficult to depend on and can be misleading.

KAREN DEYOUNG: At the Washington Post, I get a lot of the same types of calls from people, calling from all over the country, who say, "I'm going to El Salvador; tell me everything I need to know." I think you are absolutely right about the confusion that results from the different stories in the same paper. One of the things that is frustrating to me at the Post is that, unlike the New York Times, we have a three-way division between diplomatic coverage and national coverage and foreign coverage. Everybody who works on the foreign stories works someplace else. I don't have any reporters here in the U.S. They are out there in the field. They write one thing, the White House reporters write something else, the State Department reporters write another thing, and sometimes what the other two groups write is news to us and I'm sure what we write is news to them. We have the same problem, also, as has been pointed out, with the editorials relating to the information in the news columns; they sometimes build on our news stories, but sometimes they contradict them.

Another thing I want to say is that despite my comment about how we have devoted additional resources, we're still lacking in people and space in the newspaper to write about what is going on inside the Nicaraguan government, aside from who blew up what bridge. We've looked inside that government and have tried time and time again. We send people down there; they are there two days, then something happens in El Salvador, and they rush off because it is a twenty minute plane flight. Some of our people here say: "We spend $150,000 per year on this bureau so why should we have to do fifty-eight pieces on El Salvador everytime something happens?" That kind of internal allocation of time and money, and personnel and space takes a long time to sort out.

This issue comes up time and time again. We focus so much on the one story of the moment. It's not that we don't talk about Central America, but it is El

Salvador that gets the play now and only a little bit
here and there on Guatemala and the other parts of
Central America. I think more has to be done on taking
the broader, regional view and doing the follow-up.
the problem for all of us in the news business is that
we have to justify doing each story at a particular
time. But there is also room for the update story on
an issue that you have been covering over time, because
people should have some basis for knowing what the
issues are. You can come back to it much more easily.
Being able to look ahead and also to do the follow-up
of stories that we spent so much time on and then had
to drop is important.

SERGIO MOTTA MELLO: Even if you have a news bank, in
order to go beyond hard news, you have to have the
editorial decision to go. Especially television, which
is much more expensive, requires more complex
planning. You have to send crews there, you have to
have the technical facilities to send the pictures and
information at the same time. Sometimes you can do a
story and not have the space to air it.

DONALD KIRK: I just want to point out the difficulty in
getting people to read these stories once we get to
them. I don't think anyone in this world wants to read
a 1,200 word story about Nicaraguan politics except for
six people in Washington who follow Nicaraguan internal
politics.

DON CRITCHFIELD: If those six people are on the Senate
foreign relations committee, then it is worth doing the
story. The economics of journalism you touched on, but
most of my news experience has been in the field, in
the Nicaraguan revolution and the Salvadoran situation
and in Vietnam and not from trying to cover the
perspective of Washington. To get our people in New
York to send us to Nicaragua or to El Salvador when
there is no crisis is very difficult. Once we're
there, we have to compete for a piece of that
twenty-two minutes of news on the nightly program. Not
counting commercials, that's twenty-two minutes of
news, domestic and foreign. That's about nine things
happening in the world today, folks. In competition
with all the other news around the world, I have to get
in my one minute, thirty seconds. A minute and thirty
seconds is all I can have; at the height of the
revolution in Nicaragua, maybe, we got two and a half
minutes on the air.
        Nicaragua was, I think, the first revolution ever
covered by the electronic media where we were on every
night through the fall of the government without
missing a beat. One of these days, once the satellites

begin working, we're going to be out in the middle of El Salvador taking pictures of a fire-fight and sending it back home. I don't know if that makes it more horrible or whether the viewers will simply see it as another version of "Starsky and Hutch" and watch the mayhem and wonder if all the "victims" will just get up off the ground by the time we've finished the next commercial.

PAT ELLIS: One positive thing that you said about television coverage and something we can zero in on more is the fact that television brings you into direct contact with the primary sources for a story. It's not only pictures of war that you can get. You can also get to the basic sources and the key people involved in any big issue, when they are willing to speak. Obviously, it is not always when you want them to speak, but sometimes the requirements of the story and their willingness to speak can be made to mesh. I think this is very important in helping people to get information and gain a better understanding and come to their own conclusions about what they want to believe.

JIM LOBE: One of the things which has been touched on by practically everybody is the problem of limited space and the fact that reporters are always competing for it. When there isn't an election going on, or when there isn't a certification crisis, or when there isn't a battle to film, your editors just aren't going to be interested in running your story. There may be some very important, but quiet, political or diplomatic developments taking place, but if they aren't in the nature of a public crisis, it's tough to get space.
     That problem related directly as well to the attitude of the diplomatic press corps in Washington and the daily noon briefing at the State Department where, as Jeff Biggs said a few minutes ago, U.S. policy is made public.
     If the prestige media -- or the eastern establishment press, as Jeff called it -- does not consider an event in El Salvador as a crisis, it is very difficult to get it addressed publicly by the State Department. It runs the show. Its members sit in the front and control the briefing. When they want the briefing finished, it is very difficult to ask questions on issues in which they're not interested. They generally reflect traditional U.S. foreign policy concerns, which means that they are most concerned with Europe, the Middle East and U.S.-Soviet relations. There can be any number of questions asked about these areas, and they're all permitted, and nobody up front gets terribly impatient.
     That isn't what happens if you raise a question

about Central America -- or about most other parts of
the Third World, for that matter -- unless it relates
to a specific crisis that has already been reported in
the prestige media. Then their reaction very often is:
"Oh God, not El Salvador again." The pressure is to
shut up and not to mention it, to go directly to staff
people at the Department later -- or let the matter
drop. It is a very intimidating process.

The result does a double disservice, I think.

First, I don't get an on-the-record comment on
events in which my readers may be interested. More
important, however, the prestige media -- which do so
much to set the public agenda on foreign policy issues
-- does not itself hear about the quieter events
between crises -- the gaps as Jeff called them -- that
may shape U.S. policy and subsequently produce the next
crisis which results in all the cameras being sent to
El Salvador once again.

This impatience by the prestige media for
questions and information about El Salvador, or Central
America, results not only in less sustained attention
to that region of the world on the part of the prestige
media and gneeral public opinion. It also re-inforces
the public image of El Salvador, Central America, and
much of the Third World nas places that are
crisis-prone and where events take place that are
irrational, illogical, lacking in understandable cause
and effect, and always seem to come from out of the
blue.

DAN JAMES: Before we close, I want to come back to the
question of whether the media had identified the
Marxist character of the Salvadoran guerillas. The
answer is: no, not adequately.

Has anyone seen, either published in the print
media or televised, a program on the Salvadoran
communist party, on the goals and policies of the
so-called liberation front? Of all the many programs
on the guerillas I have yet to see any serious
treatment of their Marxist ideology. This is a story
that has been totally omitted. Instead, the media have
belabored the point that the guerillas allegedly want a
"democratic revolutionary government." This is not a
program of the FMLN. I can refer you to its own
documentation. This is one of the many important
stories that the media have omitted, and which we have
not talked about here. If you are reporting on a
guerilla movement, if you are talking about a so-called
civil war, then you are obliged to describe what the
rebels stand for. What does the FMLN stand for? From
reading or listening to the news, I wouldn't know.

DAVID NEWSOM: This is not a foreign agents registration

act termination of a conversation, but I want to say on behalf of the Institute we thank you for a very stimulating occasion. I'm sure we'll hear a lot more about the issues we have discussed here today.

LANDRUM BOLLING: And I want to thank Dan James for being willing to take on what is inevitably a kind of "fall guy" role and starting us off on a very provocative discussion.

5
Published Critiques of Media Coverage of Central America

Covering the Sandinistas:
The Foregone Conclusions of the Fourth Estate
By Shirley Christian

Tomas Borge is a very important man in Nicaragua. He is the only surviving founder of the Sandinista National Liberation Front. A Marxist who spent most of his adult years in the bush before reaching power, he is Fidel Castro's oldest friend and Muammar Gaddafi's newest friend in Nicaragua.

In the nearly three years since Anastasio Somoza Debayle fled the country and the Sandinistas took power, Tomas Borge has become one of the most important of the former guerrilla commanders who now run Nicaragua -- the Sandinista Front. His empire is the Interior Ministry which includes the security police. Younger members of his faction organize the neighborhood defense committees -- a kind of cross section between the PTA and the Ku Klux Klan.

It is Borge and his people who killed one business leader, who throw others into jail for criticizing the government, who send mobs to attack the newspaper La Prensa and radio news programs they do not like and keep Nicaragua in a state of disruption with their regular charges of plots allegedly afoot against the government.

Among students of Latin American guerrilla movements, Borge has achieved an almost mythical stature in the last two decades. And yet, the Washington Post, the New York Times and CBS television barely mentioned him in their coverage of the Nicaraguan insurrection in 1978 and 1979.

Despite Borge's historical importance to the Sandinista movement since its beginnings, reporting by correspondents from these three news organizations

Reprinted from the Washington Journalism Review, March 1982 by permission of the author.

virtually ignored him as a potential post-Somoza power. Nor was Borge's Marxist ideology, or that of most of the other top Sandinistas, given much attention in the few stories they wrote about the kind of government that would succeed Somoza.

The important news of the insurrection, as reported by the American press, was not Tomas Borge or others like him. The issue was Anastasio Somoza Debayle, the corruption and cruelty of a regime that had stayed in power too long. Somoza was easy to hate. When he cried wolf -- that communists were trying to take over Nicaragua -- reporters either contradicted him or said it simply did not matter. His opponents, by contrast, seemed -- at least in their public face -- easy to love. Tomas Borge was only rarely part of that public face as it was reported by correspondents for American newspapers and television.

Why did the American press fail to see the coming importance of Tomas Borge and others like him? Did American newspaper and television reporters, in their acknowledged enthusiasm for ridding Central America of Somoza, misrepresent the Sandinistas to the American public, or in other ways fail their obligations as objective reporters?

To find out, I studied 244 <u>Washington Post</u> stories, 239 <u>New York Times</u> stories and 156 CBS broadcasts on Nicaragua from January 1, 1978 to July 21, 1979. The time frame opens with the assassinatin of Pedro Joaquin Chamorro, publisher of <u>La Prensa</u>, which was a major event in unifying Somoza's opponents. It closes with the Sandinistas taking power.

First, some personal disclaimers: Nicaragua was not my war. I was living in Chile which is farther, geographically and culturally, from Nicaragua than almost any corner of the United States. I had not previously read or heard the coverage of Nicaragua by the <u>Times</u>, the <u>Post</u> and CBS. I approached this critique somewhat like the juror who has not previously read or heard accounts of the case she is about to try.

I have, however, been covering Nicaragua since Somoza fell and the Sandinistas came to power, and I have been covering civil wars and guerrilla movements elsewhere in Central America. As a result, much of what I say constitutes as much a soul-searching of my own work as an analysis and criticism of the work of others. It is done, I admit, with the brilliance of hindsight and without any particular scientific expertise. Finally, I do not know whether I would have done it differently or better had I been there.

Some cool-minded historian of the future will undoubtedly conclude that Somoza got a raw deal from the foreign correspondents who covered his downfall. Somoza said his National Guard was fighting a bunch of communists, and he turned out to be partly right. He said Panama's Omar Torrijos was shipping them arms and men, and he turned out to be right. He said the president of Venezuela was sending arms and ammunition, and he turned out to be right. He said his democratic neighbor, Costa Rica, was giving the guerrillas bed and board and tender loving care, and he turned out to be right. Finally, he said that Cuba, too, had jumped in with weapons and ammunition, and he turned out to be right.

A future revisionist historian, however, will not have known this third, and last, member of the Somoza family to reign over Nicaragua or why reporters came to hate him. Somoza did not do the things that traditionally make reporters hostile. He was, by the standards of most national leaders, extremely accessible to foreign correspondents. (One reporter who covered the war in Nicaragua for an American wire service told me he could get Somoza on the telephone in five minutes, day or night.) Nor was access to the war's battlefronts restricted. The only limits on a reporter covering Somoza's war were courage, time and initiative.

The American press disliked Somoza because of the corrupt way they had seen him run the country for years and because he was Somoza. A big, blustery man who spoke in World War II American slang, he used anti-communism as his rallying cry and bought everyone around him. He was called, disparagingly, "the Last Marine," in a country that was once a United States Marine fiefdom. Add the brutality of his National Guard, witnessed by American reporters during his last year in power, and you have a kind of leader that 99 percent of American reporters cannot stomach.

The antagonism of American reporters towards Somoza was no secret. In May 1978, Somoza's public relations representative in Washington wrote a letter to the New York Times accusing Alan Riding, the Times correspondent in Nicaragua, of trying to be the "Herbert Matthews" of Nicaragua -- a reference to the Times correspondent of twenty-five years ago who searched out Fidel Castro and his small band of guerrillas in the Sierra Maestra and, some think, resurrected Castro's cause.

Given this press hatred, by no means limited to Riding, it perhaps was not surprising that reporters covering the war saw Somoza's opponents, the Sandinistas, through a romantic haze. This romantic view of the Sandinistas is by now acknowledged publicly or privately by virtually every American journalist who was in Nicaragua during the two big Sandinista offensives, the general strikes and the various popular uprisings. Probably not since Spain has there been a more open love affair between the foreign press and one of the belligerents in a civil war.

That was the mood of the time. Since then, the mood has changed abruptly. There have been many anguished second thoughts both inside Nicaragua and in Washington about the Marxism of the Sandinistas, about whether their victory could have been prevented, whether their policies and goals can now be modified.

How the Sandinistas and other opponents of Somoza were described ideologically is not the only standard by which to judge American press coverge of the period, but given the controversy that has since arisen about the government now in power in Nicaragua, it would seem to be the central one. This is not to suggest that American reporters should constantly drum home that a political or guerrilla figure is Marxist and has ties to Cuba. It is to say that these are elements that cannot be ignored or lightly dismissed.

There was remarkable similarity in the tone of the reporting in the New York Times and the Washington Post on the ideology of the Sandinistas. (CBS did not take up the ideology issue seriously until a month before the Sandinistas took power in mid-1979.)

Neither the Times nor the Post denied or ignored the Marxist roots and Cuban ties of the Sandinista Front since its founding in 1962. There was a distinct tendency, however, to stress the reassuring impression that the Sandinista movement had been taken over in recent years by non-Marxists, many of them the sons and daughters of the bourgeosie who had become guerrillas after seeing their parents frustrated in their efforts to defeat Somoza peacefully. Faced with this, the Marxist oldtimers in the movement had supposedly given up their plans for installing a socialist state immediately after taking power. The sources quoted on this trend were primarily the non-Marxists themselves, most of whom are now in exile or otherwise disillusioned with the government.

Riding of the Times, who was probably the most informed on the Sandinista structure and the movement's internal disputes, explained in an analytical piece on May 14, 1978: "Ironically, the current offensive against the regime began last fall after a faction of the country's guerrillas, known as the Sandinist(sic) National Liberation Front, concluded that they alone could not overthrow General Somoza. They there abandoned their immediate objective of bringing socialism to Nicaragua and formed a loose alliance with numerous non-Marxist groups that were also disenchanted with the corruption and repression of the Government, agreeing to work together for the ouster of the regime and the establishment of democracy."

Riding went on to say that the so-called

"Tercerista" faction, which included most of the non-Marxists, had in recent months seen the protest movement slip from its hands and into the control of the more radical factions, the Prolonged Popular War group (headed by Tomas Borge) and the Proletarian group. These groups, he said, were "placing the battle against the regime clearly within the broader context of a 'class struggle.'"

But later, in a _Times_ Sunday magazine article in July, 1978, Riding ignored the importance of two other groups and wrote a finely detailed story of how the Terceristas whose leaders, the Ortesa brothers, were themselves Marxists, had made their appeal to non-Marxists. He also told how those people, in turn, had formed an alliance with a respected group of business and professional men of center and center-left views. The latter group, known as the Twelve, was later to supply several Cabinet ministers and two junta members to the Sandinista government.

In a passage that explains why many moderates were attracted to that alliance, Riding wrote: "In May 1977, the well-to-do lawyer, Joaquin Cuadra Chamorro, flew to Honduras for a secret meeting with his son, the guerrilla officer. 'He explained to me that socialism was not immediately possible, and that struck me as sensible and realistic,' the older man recalled. 'He said the guerrillas wanted to ally themselves with other groups and that I could play a role. So we reached an agreement with the clear understanding that socialism was not possible for Nicaragua. I saw my role as trying to rescue our youth from radicalism.'"

Karen DeYoung, who did most of the reporting from Nicaragua for the _Washington Post_, gave this explanation of the Sandinistas a few months later, on September 25, 1978: "Somoza has generated some nervousness in such countries as the United States by calling the Sandinistas terrorists and communists, bent on turning Nicaragua into another Cuba. The Sandinistas, however, have never been terrorists in the mold of the Red Brigades or Baader-Meinhof gang.

"Rather, they are revolutionaries in the Cuban sense whose activities have been politically oriented and directed toward Somoza and the National Guard.

"At the same time, it is not at all certain, despite their open advocacy of a socialist government, that the Sandinistas have either the will or the power to effect that transition rapidly. They have maintained fairly close contact with the conservative political opposition and say they would participate in a democratic government."

The following month DeYoung gained access to a Sandinista training camp and wrote three widely acclaimed articles. In one of them, carried on the front page of the <u>Post</u> under the headline, "Sandinistas Disclaim Marxism," she wrote: "Sandinista political leaders interviewed here recently denied that they are Marxists. They denied that they want Cuban-style communism in Nicaragua. Instead, they said, they are fighting for a 'new Nicaragua' that will be a 'pluralistic democracy' built on the ashes of the destroyed Somoza dictatorship."

As for Tomas Borge, the Sandinista Marxist and father figure who has been so prominent since the change of government, the brief mentions of him by both newspapers during the war period could be counted on the fingers of one hand.

When he was named to the cabinet of the provisional government a few days before Somoza fled, Riding wrote: "Only one Cabinet member, Tomas Borge, named to be minister of the interior, is a leader of the Sandinista National Liberation Front. The sources said that as head of the 'prolonged popular war' faction of the guerrilla movement, Mr. Borge should be in a position to control the most radical elements among the rebels."

DeYoung wrote on the same day: "Perhaps the most interesting on the list is the Sandinista leader Tomas Borge as interior minister. Borge, a self-declared Marxist, is considered a pragmatist. He heads the Prolonged Popular War faction...

"As interior minister, political analysts said, Borge will also serve as director of police functions and thus will be in a better position to keep mavericks from his faction in line."

CBS generally dealt with the question of the Sandinistas' ideology in simplistic terms -- referring to them in passing as leftwing or Marxist guerrillas or even terrorists -- until June 14, 1979, when Dan Rather began a morning news commentary by asking, "Who are these guys?"

After tracing the charges of Cuban or Soviet connections, he said: "The Sandinistas themselves flatly deny that they are Communists. 'Yes,' their leadership says, 'there may be Communists among us. But,' they say, 'there are also many among us dedicated to representative democracy as practiced in the United States.'"

The question, Rather concluded, was not easy to answer.

In the coming days, CBS took longer looks at the Sandinista movement, including discussions between Marvin Kalb, CBS State Department correspondent in Washington, and various correspondents in the field. In general, Kalb, perhaps reflecting the concerns of many in the U.S. government, was more suspect of the Sandinistas' motives, while those in the field were more open-minded. (These discussions, it should be noted, followed by a few days the killing of ABC correspondent Bill Stewart by a member of Somoza's National Guard, an event that had further solidified the animosity of foreign journalists toward Somoza, even though the shooting had obviously been outside his control.)

On Thursday morning, July 19, 1979, the day Nicaragua officially fell to the Sandinistas, Bob Schieffer asked Chuck Gomez in Managua whether he agreed with Kalb's assessment that the "new group" coming in was Marxist. Gomez replied that it was "inaccurate, at best" and as proof pointed to the many non-Marxists who had been named to posts in the new government. They included two of the five members of what was to become the governing junta and the majority of the cabinet.

I do not suggest that journalists on the scene in Nicaragua intentionally misled their readers about what the Sandinistas were or would become. Much of the difficulty lay in understanding the amorphous nature of the opposition to Somoza. As Alan Riding wrote early on, it was a national mutiny more than anything else. The Sandinistas were the only ones in the mutiny who had guns. The others -- businessmen, labor unions, political parties, the church leadership -- made so much noise and played such a dominant role in the mediation attempts that it was easy for most reporters to assume they would share power when the revolution was over. Most of the sources quoted in the _Post_ and the _Times_ about the nature of the Sandinistas or the likely future government were not Marxists, but members of the so-called moderate or conservative opposition to Somoza, most of whom, significantly, have since broken with the government. Some have left the country altogether; others are now internal dissidents.

The most startling example is Eden Pastora, the famous Sandinista leader during the war, the man who caught the world's attention when, as "Commander Zero," he captured the National Palace in August, 1978 and bargained the lives of more than 1,500 hostages to win freedom from prison for Tomas Borge and a number of other Sandinista guerrillas.

The stories of the war period that I analyzed inevitably described the charismatic Pastora as the main guerrilla leader, almost ignoring the shadowy presence of the nine other top commanders. It was the nine others who eventually were named to the unified directorate -- formed at the insistence of Fidel Castro, who also reportedly insisted that Pastora be excluded.

Presumbably this was because Pastora, as he told many journalists who interviewed him, was not a

Marxist. The Washington Post once described him, in his
own words, as a conservative Roman Catholic. When
DeYoung visited him at his camp, he told her he wanted
to lead a Nicaraguan government modeled after Costa
Rica's social democracy and said the only thing he had
in common with Castro was that both had been educated
by Jesuits.

Today, Pastora is in exile. He had very little
power in the new government and left Managua last July
under mysterious circumstances. Though the Sandinista
Front suggested he had gone off to fight on behalf of
guerrillas elsewhere, stronger evidence indicates that
he has been in Costa Rica, Panama and Venezuela trying
to make up his mind whether to challenge his former
colleagues for control of Nicaragua.

Aside from Pastora, the overwhelming majority of
sources quoted by CBS, the Post and the Times about the
nature of the rebels were the business leaders,
opposition politicians, professionals, and
intellectuals who were, by their own admission, hoping
to wean the Sandinista Front away from its
Marxist-Leninist ideology and had no idea whether they
would succeed. The man, for example, who was regularly
called upon to respond to charges of Cuban involvement
with the Sandinistas was millionaire industrialist
Alfonso Robelo, who was probably not even taken into
the Sandinistas' confidence about the subject.

This raises questions about the difficulties
confronting journalists who cover guerrilla wars and
popular front movements. Should such movements be
taken at face value? Does, or will, the man out in
front have real power? Or is he out in front because
he looks respectable to the West?

In Nicaragua the respectable looking Sandinista
was Pastora. Apparently not a Marxist, he was always
identified by reporters as the top guerrilla
commander. There were also moderates in the
five-member junta in exile set up by the rebels in
Costa Rica that supposedly would run the future
government. As it turned out, Pastora and his
followers were largely excluded from jobs of influence
after the victory, and the junta became little more
than an administrative organ answerable to the nine-man
Sandinista Directorate.

Much of the war coverage which I examined did not
ponder what kind of government would succeed Somoza but
dwelt instead on the brutality of his National Guard
and its bombardment of civilian areas, and on efforts
to remove him. Coming face to face with scenes and
stories of atrocities committed by the Guard apparently
made the political coloration of the Sandinista Front
seem pale by comparison.

DeYoung of the Post and various CBS correspondents

gave vivid accounts of their visits to towns and neighborhoods that had been recaptured or bombarded by the National Guard. DeYoung's reporting on killings by the National Guard in the town of Leon during the September, 1978 offensive appeared to have prompted the U.S. government to request an OAS investigation of atrocities. That investigation probably was a major factor in the rest of Latin America eventually lining up against Somoza.

DeYoung's story reported that fourteen young men had, according to family members, been executed by the National Guard as they begged for mercy.

"The eyewitnesses' story of the execution is supported by physical evidence on the scene and by countless similar reports, primarily here in Leon, of National Guard atrocities during nearly four weeks of civil war," she wrote.

Much later, as the United States government agonized over how far it should go to save part of the National Guard as a possible counterbalance to the Sandinistas in the future government, DeYoung suggested in an article on July 9, 1979 that it was not worth saving.

After writing of the daily discoveries of the bodies of young men in the tall grass on the edge of Lake Managua, she said: "President Anastasio Somoza says the National Guard does not carry out summary executions. Yet similar groups of young men -- shirtless and blindfolded -- are seen daily being marched, single file with their hands on each other's shoulders, through Managua's central jail compound."

David Dick of CBS, in a report from Masaya during the same offensive, interviewed a teacher who reported on the torture of a student by the National Guard as it tried to put down the rebellion there. "They tortured him," the teacher said. "They took his testicles, you know, with a glove, and they pressed this way, you know. After that they took some electric shocks...After that they put...the barrel of the gun in his anus, you know."

Two weeks later, Bruce Hall of CBS reported from Esteli: "Most of those killed were civilians, caught in the crossfire. There were reports of atrocities by both the National Guard and the rebels, but nothing like those in Leon last week, where the Red Cross says several hundred people many have been executed by the National Guard."

There were almost no reports by the _Post_, _Times_ and CBS of unjustified or noncombat brutality by Sandinista forces against government supporters. One paragraph in a story mentioned a charge that the Sandinistas were taking reprisals after they had captured Leon, but reported no investigation of it.

There were also brief mentions of "government informers" being killed or threatened.

One reason, undoubtedly, was that nearly all Nicaraguans gave reporters the impression of being, if not in favor of the Sandinistas, at least against the National Guard. More importantly, virtually every journalist I know who covered the war was convinced that the overwhelming share of the unnecessary violence was committed by the government troops. Everything they saw or heard first hand convinced them of that.

There is another consideration, that has to do with our capabilities as journalists to cover adequately guerrilla wars and popular insurrections. While it was undoubtedly true that the National Guard reacted with the heaviest hand imaginable, it is also apparent that the Sandinistas, by their strategy, almost invited the Guard to attack the provincial towns and the poor neighborhoods of the capital.

They used two kinds of actions. In one, a few of them with the help of local muchachos -- the sympathetic and unemployed neighborhood youth -- would actually set off the "insurrection" by setting a few fires or throwing a few small bombs. In the other, larger groups of Sandinistas would set up barricades to take over a town or neighborhood.

The Guard soon learned that it was easier to fight the Sandinistas with heavy bombardment or even bombings than face them in the streets. The result was that more civilians were killed than Sandinistas, who had the mobility to quickly withdraw when things became hot. This also meant that the civilians were left behind to bear the brunt of the Guard's aminosity when it reclaimed the area.

It may not have been intentional on the part of the Sandinistas to force civilians to suffer, but Riding suggested in an analytical piece in the Times early in 1978 that some guerrilla movements had as their objective the provoking of repression by authoritarian regimes as a means of increasing popular discontent. He suggested that the thesis had more validity among guerrilla groups in El Salvador and Guatemala and said that it had been rejected by the Sandinistas in Nicaragua. His quoted source, however, was a member of the Pastora camp.

One of the reasons the violence in Nicaragua had such an impact on reporters was that the press was much closer to the Nicaraguan war than it had been to others. Nicaragua, an agricultural nation of fewer than 2.5 million people, is somewhat like an extended small town where everybody seems to know everybody else or to be related. Most of the newspaper correspondents and some of the television people spoke Spanish at a level ranging from adequate to excellent. Some had worked in Nicaragua off and on for years and had acquaintances there on all sides of the issue. The Hispanic-Indian, Roman Catholic culture of the country was not totally foreign to them.

While stories having to do with the structure and ideas of the rebels were complex to write and difficult to obtain, those having to do with the victims of violence were more vivid and close at hand. Probably not since World War II in Europe have American correspondents felt such proximity to the victims. But in that war, news reports were censored.

I cannot help asking whether the horrors that journalists saw in Nicaragua constituted a reign of brutality and terror by an especially repressive regime or whether they were the horrors of any kind of war, seen without censorship and language and cultural barriers.

While concentrating on abuses of power by the National Guard and often linking the abuses to the arms and training the troops had long received from the United States, the _Post_, _Times_ and CBS generally paid little attention to the question of arms and ammunition reaching the Sandinistas and the assistance given them by other countries. Their reporters in Nicaragua brushed off Somoza's charges that the Sandinistas were receiving arms first from Venezuela through Panama and Costa Rica and later from Cuba.

The few times that these issues were raised by correspondents in Washington, they received only slightly more serious consideration from the three news organizations.

Yet, it would have been relatively easy to investigate the charges that the guns were coming in from the south, through Costa Rica, which is a very open place. Costa Rican congressional investigators have since uncovered vast and unchallenged evidence of wholesale gun trafficking through their country to the Nicaraguan rebels. However right the cause against Somoza and however much the Costa Rican people supported it, this was a story that demanded to be reported thoroughly -- and was not.

Reporters from some news organizations did write that Costa Rica's Guanacaste Province was virtually occupied by Sandinistas during the war. Everybody saw it who went there. Among other things, Sandinista hospitals for the war wounded operated in the area, and not in makeshift conditions but in fairly decent buildings.

Yet, the _Times_ and the _Post_ reported on the Costa Rican link only very late and in a very limited way, even though they often had correspondents in the Costa Rican capital covering the activities of the rebel junta and its negotiations with the United States. CBS, for all practical purposes, ignored the situation in northern Costa Rica.

By not digging into the gun-running charges and the rumors, even then, of flights directly from Cuba to northern Costa Rica, a major story of the war was largely missed -- the cutoff of Venezuelan guns to Pastora and his followers after the new Venezuelan president took office in March 1979 and the nearly simultaneous beginning of Castro's shipments of ammunition and guns to the Marxist factions of the Sandinista movement. This is most likely what cost Pastora a stronger hand in Nicaragua's post-war power structure.

Reporters missed or underreported other important stories of the insurrection, such as the very effective organization set up by Sandinista sympathizers to control poor Nicaraguan neighborhoods, the Sandinista lobby in Washington, and the feuding between the National Security Council and the State Department over how far the United States should go in forcing Somoza to resign during the first mediation period, in late 1978, a good six months before he finally left.

The sad truth, however, is that almost no one in the American press cared about how the Sandinistas got their supplies, or that the main foreign government source had suddenly changed from Venezuela to Cuba. The American media, like most of the United States, went on a guilt trip in Nicaragua. The U.S. government, for its part, was so burdened by half a century of mistakes in Nicaragua that it could not deal with the present. Journalists carried that guilt on the one hand, and on the other the conviction learned from Vietnam that U.S. foreign policy was never again to be trusted.

As a result, the press got on the Sandinistas' bandwagon and the story that reporters told -- with a mixture of delight and guilt -- was the ending of an era in which the United States had once again been proved wrong. Obsessed with the past, journalists were unable, or unwilling, to see the tell-tale signs of the future. Intrigued by the decline and fall of Anastasio Somoza, they could not see the coming of Tomas Borge.

Taking Exception to "Covering the Sandinistas"

Responses to an article by Shirley Christian in the March 1982, issue of Washington Journalism Review, that appeared in the May 1982 issue of WJR.

From Karen DeYoung, Foreign Editor, The Washington Post:

Since the role of the U.S. media in Nicaragua during 1978-79, as well as their current role in Central America, have been subjects of much public discussion in this country, I believe they are well worth serious exploration by the journalistic community itself. I was therefore eager to read Shirley Christian's article "Covering the Sandinistas"....

According to Ms. Christian, the research on which her article is based consists of "244 Washington Post stories, 239 New York Times stories and 156 CBS broadcasts on Nicaragua from January 1, 1978 to July 21, 1979." To bolster her conclusion that the American press did a bad, or at least naive and incomplete job in Nicaragua...Ms. Christian states that "virtually every American journalist who was in Nicaragua during the two big Sandinista offensives, the general strikes and the various popular uprisings" has since acknowledged "publicly or privately" that he or she had "a romantic view of the Sandinistas." Additionally, she says that there have been "many anguished second thoughts both inside Nicaragua and in Washington about the Sandinistas and their Marxism."

As Ms. Christian points out, nearly every article in the Washington Post written from Nicaragua during that period, and a number written from Washington, appeared under my byline. I assume...she intends my inclusion among the journalists to whom she refers. For the record, I have never acknowledged, "publicly or privately," having a "romantic view" of the Sandinistas, nor have I had second thoughts about my reporting, anguished or otherwise. I have never met nor spoken to Ms. Christian nor, to the best of my knowledge, did she make any attempt to contact me prior to publication of the article.

Because of this, and the fact she mentions my name eight times and cites passages from my articles, I feel I am entitled to, and your readers deserve, a detailed response to what I consider a failed attempt at deductive reasoning in which the overall conclusion is ill-founded, and the supporting documentation is highly selective and in many cases at variance with the facts.

The thesis of the article, subtitled "The Foregone Conclusions of the Fourth Estate" is that the U.S. media, in newspaper stories and broadcasts between January 1978 and July 1979, "were unable, or unwilling, to see the tell-tale signs of the future" and failed to tell the world what was going to happen in Nicaragua. Why? Because they viewed the Sandinista National Liberation Front through a "romantic haze" and "hated" former Nicaraguan President Anastasio Somoza.

Leaving aside for a moment the issue of whether it is possible or desirable for a journalist to predict the future, or tailor coverage perhaps even to alter the future, I would like to address the two premises on which Ms. Christian's thesis is based.

...I will assume that she assesses the Nicaragua of the "future" (i.e., the present -- what we did not tell people two years ago was coming) as a Cuba-like, Marxist state run by Tomas Borge.

It is, in fact, neither. As described by Ms. Christian's newspaper and many others, as well as any number of serious academics, U.S. government officials and Nicaraguans themselves, the Nicaraguan government is an amalgam of Marxist former guerillas of varying commitment to ideology, assisted by a group of leftist and centrist technocrats, who rule in tacit, sometimes limited, recognition that a strong private sector and relatively restricted opposition parties and press are necessary for current national viability.

Additionally, I am surprised that someone with Ms. Christian's experience in Latin America, and particularly in Nicaragua, would describe Borge as a man of "mythic stature" among Latin revolutionaries over the last two decades, and would imply that he is singularly powerful among the Sandinistas. As one of the nine members of the Sandinista directorate, and head of the interior ministry, Borge is indeed powerful. He is not all powerful, nor even considered the most powerful among the nine (nor, for that matter, is he even considered the "most Marxist" among them...). Nor is he the most widely known of the Sandinista leaders among other Latin American revolutionaries.

Ms. Christian notes that "the most startling example" of a failure to understand who the real Marxist Sandinista powers were, was the description and use as a source of Eden Pastora. "The stories of the war period that I analysed," she says, inevitably described the charismatic Pastora as the main guerilla leader, almost ignoring the shadowy presence of the nine other top commanders. It was the nine others who eventually were named to the unified directorate -- formed at the insistence of Fidel Castro, who also reportedly insisted that Pastora be excluded." Later, Ms. Christian says Pastora "was always indentified by reporters as the top guerilla commander."

In re-reading every article I wrote during the cited period, I find no reference to Pastora as the main guerilla leader. As was well known, and written repeatedly by myself and others, Pastora was a military leader; he had little or no political power in the FSLN. On Oct. 19, 1978, I called Pastora the "undisputed military commander of the Sandinista troops, their chief tactician...." Fresh from his triumph at the National Palace, there is no question that Pastora was the best known of the Sandinistas, inside and outside Nicaragua. Neither is there any question that he was, and continued to be the principal military commander and tactician. But not even he himself claimed to be a political power or policy-maker within the movement or to be in agreement with those who were.

The Oct. 19 article, a profile of Pastora, noted that Pastora himself was imbued with his newfound notoriety, and said, in what appeared to be partial jest, that he wanted to be president of Nicaragua. "More experienced as a military strategist than a politician," it goes on, "Pastora does not suffer from lack of confidence in either field." He notes that some Sandinistas have been trained in Cuba, and says that while many Sandinistas are Marxists, he is not. He claims he would like to see democracy in Nicaragua, although he has no doubt the more extreme ideologues among the Sandinistas have no intention of laying down their guns. The profile concludes: "Compared to recognized Sandinista political leaders, Pastora appears to have little ideology beyond the eventual installation of a democratic government, which he hopes to lead."

I made little further mention of Pastora until June 18, 1979, when I discussed him briefly as "the guerilla chief of military operations who staged a successful raid on Managua's National Palace." In my description of the new government on July 22 (which I realize is one day after Ms. Christian's reading cutoff) I wrote "one of the best known names among the Sandinistas, Eden Pastora, known as Commander Zero, has not been given a place in the leadership but will remain in the army...although well known, he is not a major political force."

...I wonder why Ms. Christian refers to the "shadowy" presence of the nine themselves. Their names were well known, they were frequently mentioned, and I personally interviewed and used as sources Daniel Ortega, Victor Manuel Tirado, Humberto Ortega, and Jaime Wheelock among them during 1978 and 1979. Neither their identities, their backgrounds, their ideologies nor their power was secret or unreported. During the same period, I spoke with Eden Pastora a total of one time -- on the occasion of the above-mentioned profile.

My two-part series of articles dated Oct. 24-25, 1978, to which Ms. Christian refers, made ample mention of the Cuban-inspired origins of the Sandinistas, the reasons for the split among them (tactics rather than ideology) and their longterm commitment to socialism. An April 5, 1979 story described the split in more detail. Another two-part series beginning on June 24, 1979, described the origin, splits, unity and ideology yet again, as well as the Cuban and PLO training a number of the Sandinistas received.

Lest it appear I am using selected portions of my own articles to subscribe to Ms. Christian's (unstated) thesis that Nicaragua is a Cuban-run totalitarian state, I should point out that those same articles, and many others, describe the Sandinistas before their victory as building popular support from the poor villages and barrios of Nicaragua, through most political parties, every union and business organization and virtually every other sector of Nicaraguan society. Reporting that support was not part of an effort by any reporter to make the Sandinistas appear "moderate" or more popular than Somoza, or to disguise the Marxism of their leadership. It was very real, and was reported as such.

Similarly reported were Sandinista efforts to fill their pre-victory provisional government with civilians who were viewed by Latin American allies and the United States as acceptably moderate and U.S. government efforts to change the makeup of that government on grounds that it was too heavily weighted toward Marxists. To my knowledge, none of the "moderates" who were brought into the government had, by the end of July, 1979, expressed a feeling, belief or knowledge that their power and input into decision-making would be unacceptably limited. Some of them later said this, and left the government. Some of them have not. In several articles during the last two weeks of July, 1979, I analyzed the new government and the potential for problems -- among them the belief of many Sandinistas that they were the only true power in the country, the difficult transformation from guerillas to government, and the historical failure (as in post-war Eastern Europe) of coalition governments with the far left. To "ponder" the future, as Ms. Christian puts it, beyond this was the job of editorialists and writers of opinion. How the Nicaraguan drama subsequently was played out was a subject for later coverage by correspondents like Ms. Christian.

Ms. Christian also cites press "hatred" for and "dislike" of Somoza as one of the principal reasons for what she says was the press' inability to look realistically at what was happening in Nicaragua, or to look into the post-Somoza future. Since no articles in the New York Times or the Washington Post are cited to support this description of attitude (with the exception of one reference to a letter written by Somoza's press agent to the Times), nor can I find any in my own reading, I wonder where this after-the-fact notion came from.

I regret that a journalist of Ms. Christian's stature would appear to have confused the messenger with the message.

The reporting of the fact that Somoza was not
popular with most Nicaraguans, nor with any of the
world's democracies, had nothing to do with whether
reporters themselves liked or disliked Somoza, any more
than the downfall of South Vietnamese President Thieu,
or Salvadoran President Romero, or the Shah of Iran or
Cambodia's Pol Pot had any discernible relationship to
the way reporters "felt" about them. They fell because
their military forces were defeated or gave up and/or
their people decided to get rid of them and/or they
lost outside support on which their power depended --
all of which applied to Somoza.

I conducted and reported extensive interviews with
Somoza on at least half a dozen occasions during the
period cited, including the last interview he gave
before leaving Nicaragua. In addition, I spoke with him
frequently on the telephone and attended all the press
conferences he gave. I would challenge Ms. Christian
to find a passage in my reporting that "contradicted
him" without facts or "said it simply did not matter."
Although his various press agents, and a later
ghost-written book, blamed the press for some of his
troubles, Somoza was very specific, as reported in the
various interviews cited above. He blamed the Carter
administration -- in particular former Secretary of
State Cyrus Vance and Assistant Secretary William
Bowdler -- Fidel Castro, former Venezuelan President
Carlos Andres Perez, the late Panamanian head of state
Omar Torrijos as well as what he felt was a naive and
traitorous Nicaraguan business community and the
Sandinistas themselves.

In that last interview, Somoza told me he had only
two complaints about the press -- the Washington Post
in particular. He objected to an editorial recently
printed, about which I told him I had no knowledge or
control, and the fact that I had written that "nobody
liked the National Guard." I told him that during
several years' travelling around Nicaragua I had yet to
meet a Nicaraguan not in his or the National Guard's
employ who had a good thing to say about his armed
forces. If he could direct me to some, I would report
them.

Ms. Christian additionally asserts that "Reporters
missed or underreported other important stories of the
insurrection, such as the very effective organization
set up by Sandinista sympathizers to control poor
Nicaraguan neighborhoods." I cannot believe that a
conscientious reporter would have overlooked my stories
on June 2, June 10, June 12 and June 25, 1979, among
others, which describe the underground neighborhood
organizations, how they operated, and the crucial role
they played during the final uprising.

Ms. Christian says that reporters "brushed off"

charges concerning arms supplies to the Sandinistas.
Yet there were repeated references, in my stories and
those of others, to arms shipped and shipments
facilitated by Venezuela, Panama, Costa Rica and Cuba,
and the Arabs, among others. There was no reason to
brush off facts that none of these governments denied.
"It would have been relatively easy to investigate the
charges that the guns were coming in from the south,
through Costa Rica," Ms. Christian says. It was, as I
reported on July 4, 1979, from Costa Rica. By the same
token, there was no need to brush off, or extensively
investigate, reports and charges that the Somoza
government, following the cutoff of U.S. military
assistance, received arms from Israel, Guatemala and
Taiwan.

Perhaps most puzzling is her contention that,
because many of the correspondents who covered the
Nicaraguan violence knew Spanish well, were familiar
with the Nicaraguan culture and had many friends on
"all sides of the issue" in Nicaragua, Ms. Christian
says, they covered the war "from a more personal level
than wars in Third World countries where the language
and culture are more unfamiliar to Americans. It was as
easy to go among the people in Nicaragua and find out
what was happening to them as it is in say, Cincinnati.

> While stories having to do with the
> structure and ideas of the rebels were
> complex to write and difficult to obtain,
> those having to do with the victims of
> violence were more vivid and close at hand.
> Probably not since World War II in Europe
> have American correspondents felt such
> proximity to the victims. But in that war,
> news reports were censored.
> I cannot help asking whether the horrors
> that journalists saw in Nicaragua constituted
> a reign of brutality and terror by an
> especially repressive regime or whether they
> were the horrors of any kind of war, seen
> without censorship and language and cultural
> barriers.

I find these comments truly astounding. Although
foreign correspondents have long been accused of
misreporting because they have little knowledge of the
countries they cover, this is the first time I have
seen the opposite charge made. As detailed above, I
believe there was substantial coverage of the structure
and ideas of the rebels. For the rest, does Ms.
Christian seriously mean to imply that the American
public was worse off for knowing about what was
happening in Nicaragua as they could expect to know

about Cincinnati during similar upheavals? Or that reporters were derelict in telling them? Or that we should gauge our reporting of "horrors" and "brutality" by whether a place is in the Third World -- rather than Cincinnati? Or would she prefer a simpler form of censorship?

In trying to support her case that journalism failed, Ms. Christian says that "much of the war coverage which I examined did not ponder what kind of government would succeed Somoza, but dwelt instead on the brutality of his national guard and its bombardment of civilian areas." While I do not know the extent of Ms. Christian's experience, to my mind the term "war coverage" means covering the war. Wars are made up of bombardments, brutality and efforts to win.

I have written at such length because I believe that to let Ms. Christian's article go unchallenged is to do a serious disservice -- or rather to compound the disservice she has already done -- to journalism, Central America and public discussion of U.S. foreign policy. In no instance does Ms. Christian clearly state her thesis, or support it with accurate and pertinent data. Instead, she has chosen...to write a polemic....

Ms. Christian concludes: "The press got on the Sandinistas' bandwagon and the story that reporters told -- with a mixture of delight and guilt -- was the ending of an era..."

The delight was the opportunity to cover an important and historically important story. The guilt was non-existent. The Sandinistas overthrew the government of Anastasio Somoza, with the suport of the vast majority of the Nicaraguan people and much of the world community. Since Ms. Christian now covers Central America, her job has been to tell what happened next.

From Alan Riding, _The New York Times_, Mexico:

Rather than "Covering the Sandinistas," I would have thought "Who Lost Nicaragua?" a better title for Shirley Christian's article....And she concludes, as is now fashionable, that the correspondents of the _New York Times_, the _Washington Post_ and a bunch of other naive romantics were in good measure responsible.

But her article is based upon several shaky premises...

Tomas Borge...is not the strongman that Shirley portrays him to be. He is one of nine members of the Sandinista National Directorate and, in no sense, the most powerful, although he does have a thirst for publicity which some reporters all too readily satisfy. Yet Shirley builds her entire argument around the fact that we "could not see the coming of Tomas Borge." It does seem odd to be charged with failing to forecast an event that has not happened. Shirley has no compunction in pronouncing Nicaragua to be a Cuban-style dictatorship even though the fight for political pluralism and a mixed economy is still very much alive.

It is true that most correspondents covering Nicaragua felt little sympathy for the Somoza dynasty -- just as few can find it in them to sympathize with El Salvador's junta -- but is this surprising? During its forty-year reign, it brought Nicaragua neither development nor democracy, two values that journalists presumably can support. Most journalists covering the revolution also reflected sympathy for the Sandinistas, but is this surprising? In the weeks preceding their victory, the rebels enjoyed the support and admiration of an entire nation. We therefore did not invent the hope that they generated among the Nicaraguans; we merely reported it. And when many Nicaraguans subsequently felt disenchanted, we reported that too. But was it really our duty to predict, say, in 1978, what Nicaragua would look like in 1982? If so, I would very much like to hear Shirley's predictions for Central America in 1986.

Finally, I was particularly puzzled by Shirley's implication that language abilities and experience of some correspondents actually distorted their coverage. Is it better to see events in the Third World through the eyes of a freshman reporter who speaks only English? And did she really intend to suggest that Somoza's "reign of terror" did not merit particular attention because, after all, war is hell? I am sure she would not apply these criteria to her own reporting of the area.

Shirley Christian replies:

Since Karen DeYoung's letter is nearly as long as my article which dealt with far more than the work of one person, there is no way I can respond to all of her comments. I would like, however, to refer to a few of the points made by her and by Alan Riding. First, it was not my unstated thesis that Nicaragua is a Cuban-run totalitarian state. I do not believe that has happened in Nicaragua, although I do believe that most of the top Sandinista leadership would accept such a system. Second, she and Alan suggest I was criticizing reporters for their knowledge of Nicaragua and their ability to speak Spanish. I did not say that in the sense of criticism but rather to help explain the depth of feeling involved in the reporting. Nor do I believe that the U.S. public was worse off as the

result. What I believe is that the public was worse
off because the same kind of close-up digging reporting
was not applied to other issues in the Nicaraguan war.
Finally, I do not expect that reporters be prophets of
the future, but I do expect us to raise more questions
and be more skeptical than occured in Nicaragua.

The State of Press Freedom in Sandinist Nicaragua
By Allen Weinstein

Six American journalists and a lawyer returned
recently from a tour of Nicaragua, El Salvador and
Guatemala arranged by a group known as "The Committee
to Protect Journalists," whose honorary chairman is
Walter Cronkite.

None of us could be considered a specialist in
Central American affairs. Our group included Jonathan
Larsen of Life magazine; George Watson of ABC News;
Randolph Ryan, an editorial writer for the Boston
Globe; Gloria Emerson, formerly a reporter for the New
York Times; and Michael Massing, executive editor of
the Columbia Journalism Review. I was acompanied by my
wife, a Washington attorney who is fluent in Spanish.

The group returned with a report that condemned
the jailing, assault and murder of press figures in El
Salvador and Guatemala. The report criticized the
guerrilla left as well as rightists for the periodic
acts of violence directed against journalists. And the
report denounced both the total repression of the free
press in Nicaragua under Sandinista rule and the many
threats to the physical safety of journalists in that
country. No sterner indictment of that regime's abuse
of press freedom has appeared in this country.

The status of the press in Nicaragua, alas, failed
to interest most of the reporters who attended a New
York City press conference called by the committee.
The journalists present virtually ignored the
Nicaraguan section of the report to concentrate on El
Salvador, an understandable interest given the recent
election and the international attention on the four
Dutch journalists whose deaths remain a matter of great
controversy.

At the same time, two members of our delegation
were so uncomfortable with our group's statement on
Nicaraguan press abuses that at the press conference
they expressed their rejection of this part of the
statement, which is printed below. All of us had
agreed previously on this section after extensive

discussion during the drafting process in Central America.

The inner history of our group's arguments over the virtues and failings of Sandinista leadership need not concern us here. What matters is the report itself. A three-day round of meetings in Nicaragua was arranged for the committee by a member of the U.S. Maryknoll religious order, a woman clearly sympathetic to government perspectives. As the report indicates, a majority of the delegation found unpersuasive the efforts there of "official" journalists, radical priests and pro-government "human rights" advocates to discredit their current adversaries in Nicaragua's democratic opposition, including genuine human-rights activists and the dwindling band of independent journalists.

Indeed, correspondents in Nicaragua informed me yesterday that a La Prensa editorial writer-reporter, Roger Alonzo Ocampa, was arrested in Managua under the emergency laws on April 2 and has not been seen since then. In Mr. Alonzo's possession at the time of his arrest was a statement prepared by La Prensa's employees' union protesting the recent Sandinista decree that required all Nicaraguan workers to remain on the job during traditional Holy Week observances.

Sandinista chic remains infectious in Western countries, nowhere more obviously perhaps than in the Orwellian praise heaped upon the new tyrants of Nicaragua by the Socialist International for the Sandinistas' alleged commitment to "pluralism" and "democracy," both of which the regime is apparently eliminating as quickly as world opinion allows.

The Nicaraguan tragedy deserves at least as much attention from the press -- and the U.S. Congress -- as the question of American involvement in El Salvador. Independent journalists in Nicaragua practice their craft at peril to their continued existence as professionals. Should the Sandinistas maintain their "state of emergency" indefinitely, there will be no independent journalists left practicing there, only pro-government flacks whose numbers grow steadily.

At that point, perhaps, the Committee to Protect Journalists could send a second expeditionary force not only to Nicaragua but also to Cuba and Grenada, both omitted from its recent itinerary. Of course, once free expression has disappeared from a country and the independent press has been crushed, there exist no journalists worthy of the name in need of protection except those in jail or in exile.

The following is the portion of the committee's statement bearing on the status of the press and free expression in Nicaragua:

In Nicaragua, we found the situation of

journalists profoundly threatening. The 1979 Nicaraguan revolution, which generated the most sweeping national liberation movement in modern Central American history, has been degenerating into an uneven struggle between the Sandinista government and its opponents. Despite Sandinista commitments and promises prior to taking power that the revolutionary government would foster pluralistic and democratic institutional development, the government of Nicaragua and its military forces now rule by decree under a recently declared state of emergency.

They are challenged by a wide range of private-sector opponents -- including the independent daily newspaper, La Prensa, church officials, independent radio stations and business and professional leaders (most of these persons had participated in the revolution). They have united openly, if loosely, in a democratic opposition coalition. Several of their leaders have been prevented from leaving the country, attacked by Sandinista-sponsored mobs (called "Turbas") and subjected to arbitrary imprisonment.

Even before the state of emergency, La Prensa had been closed down six times for printing articles which violated vague and sweeping government regulations prohibiting publication of information on economic and national security matters. A restrictive press code enforced on La Prensa a wide measure of self-censorship and resulted in the periodic closing of several independent news programs and radio stations. Archbishop Obando y Bravo has been prevented from broadcasting his weekly sermon, which had been aired regularly for the past 10 years, on the sole state-run television channel. The radio station of the Catholic Church, Radio Catolica, has been closed down indefinitely and all attempts to create an independent TV channel have been rebuffed.

Today, as a result of the recent state of emergency imposed in March, all independent radio news programs have been shut down and newspapers -- La Prensa and its two government-aligned competitors -- must submit all copy for pre-censorship; those journalists opposed to the government have been harassed and even assaulted by the "Turbas." Several journalists have served jail sentences under a broadly worded "Law to Maintain Order and Public Security," passed shortly after the Sandinistas took power, which subjects violators to military jurisdiction.

Such intimidation has taken a heavy toll on news gathering and dissemination, even by La Prensa, which, under the leadership of Pedro Chamorro, is struggling to maintain its role as a beacon of free expression throughout Central America. Virtually all independent journalists to whom we spoke believe that the government has begun a drive either to emasculate through censorship or to close the few radio stations and single newspaper which today uphold the tradition of independent journalism in Nicaragua.

An observer from government comments:

"Had I spoken, I might have referred to the impact of 'pack journalism' in generating headline treatment while the analysis or trends suffers. Witness the impending elections in Bolivia which will put the 'seal of approval' on that country's turn away from dictatorship. Witness, also, the pressures of democratic Latin American nations on the remaining dictatorships. Witness the resiliency of Caribbean democracies in the face of economic hardship. These stories do not make headlines, do not grab the attention of the public or the Congress, but they are a part of the geopolitical context in which our Central American policy is formulated.
"Another somehwat related phenomenon is the decline in American news bureaus abroad, particularly in the developing world. This has come at a time when other nations, primarily Europeans but also Latin Americans and Japanese, are expanding their international operations (Reuters opened twelve new bureaus in its North American region last year and plans twenty more this year). Most American papers rely on U.S. wire services. Excellent items by Reuters, AFP, EFE, ANSA and other agencies are missed by the American public, the Congress and often the Executive."

Francis D. Gomez

6
Reflections on Media Coverage of the Third World

A fourth session in this seminar was in part devoted to a continuation of the debate on the media coverage of Third World wars and revolutions -- and the impact of that coverage on U.S. foreign policy. Excerpts from that transcript:

DAVID NEWSOM: Landrum has asked me to throw out some thoughts seeking to draw some conclusions from the three sessions that we have already had and to state some premises for our discussion. In our two seminars on the "Media and the Third World" that concentrated on revolution and conflict situations primarily in Central America and the Middle East, we did not detect any agreed conclusions. Nor did we seek to draw any. But let me as an observer suggest some possible conclusions.

First, news is where the press happens to be. Some news is inescapable because of the interest created by governmental action, because Americans are involved, because of the particularly dramatic circumstances of the event, or because of the presumed and perceived overall seriousness of the issue. For example, I think the Middle East is almost always news, because of the recognition of the high stakes that are involved and the potential confrontation between the U.S. and the Soviets. But other news is created sometimes by the individual curiosity or initiative of a reporter, or the accidental presence of press people where something suddenly happens. If you look at one area that I have been much concerned with in my diplomatic career, Africa, you'll find that Africa is only in the news when people happen to be where something is happening. Usually, only then will Africa get on the front pages, even though something is happening on the African continent all the time.

Secondly, there is no clear agreement, either within the profession or outside the profession, on what news is or what news should be. There is, some believe, a tendency within some parts of the media to concentrate on entertainment, to emphasize the dramatic and the confrontational rather than the analytical or issues of long-term significance.

Thirdly, there is today in the press a strong tendency towards skepticism regarding official U.S. policy and those foreign officials abroad who are identified with it. The opinion has been expressed in some of our sessions, and is expressed frequently elsewhere, that the press has a tendency to look more at the flaws in our friends than the flaws in our adversaries. You can perhaps call it the Watergate/Vietnam syndrome, but it is there.

Fourth, "bias in the press" is in the eye of the beholder. We are dealing in the coverage of international issues with matters that arouse intense emotions. Those who are involved on one side or the other fault the press for lack of attention and they fault the press for excessive attention. Some make charges of conspiracies within the press against certain groups or points of view. I think there is little evidence to support such charges. It is also hard to find any evidence of purposeful bias on the part of news people or editors.

Fifth, the way issues are presented is often the result of the kind of access allowed to news sources -- and the simple availability, or lack of availability, of authoritative sources. It seems, for example, to be a fact that in many revolutionary situations, or many situations of conflict, the rebels or the adversaries are more eager to present their point of view than are the people in power. Frequently, governments with which we are associated are more difficult for our media to deal with than are their revolutionary adversaries.

Now, the coverage of international events undoubtedly affects the policy makers. Whether it affects the substance of the decisions of policy makers I think is open to question, but it affects the policy process indirectly in several ways. It pushes officials to give answers. That everlasting pressure for guidance to the press spokesman to use at the noon briefing probably creates more U.S. foreign policy in a shorter space of time than any other part of the process. The coverage of the press is substantively perhaps more important and more influential on members of Congress than it may be on the policy makers themselves. But that in turn stimulates questions in the Congress and has an effect upon policy.

Media coverage also probably stands to some extent in the way of unqualified acceptance of official policy because of continual media expressions of skepticism toward foreign policy. Coverage has an effect on public opinion which in turn can affect policy but in ways which I think are difficult to define. What is the effect on the will of this nation, on the readiness of this nation to commit military forces, that comes from the visual presentation of violence, scenes of violence and conflict, on television? What is the effect in the public mind of the contrast between the ragged and open-shirted revolutionary and the well-dressed oligarch in contrasting scenes transmitted by television from Latin America? We really don't know. But there is probably some effect.

Leaks are certainly a factor in the policy machinery but we must recognize that leaks are not always leaks; sometimes they are trial balloons from the top, sometimes they are the result of diligent reporting. But concern about leaks in these last two administrations has meant that policy has been made by fewer and fewer people in the hierarchy of the administration, precisely because of the fear of leaks. The tendency now to exclude sometimes the genuine experts because you don't want to widen the circle to those that may have access to a Xerox machine becomes a significant factor. Leaks also raise the whole question of intelligence activity and covert action to a plane of national debate where it certainly was not twenty years ago.

TV has a special impact, but the limitations of time and of the budgeting of time on television makes it difficult to assess its real influence on foreign policy.

All of this is not to suggest that the media should not continue to be a major factor in the making and implementation of policy. The press does help to shape views -- of the general public and of the Congress. I think if the press is honest with itself, it finds its views are sometimes shaped, too. It's not the perfect thing. You all know that old sexist joke about the man who was asked, "how is your wife today?" and his reply was, "compared to what?" My answer to "how is the press?" is to say that the American press has its faults but, compared to the alternatives, it is a very important and desirable instrument of our policy.

NICK THIMMESCH: David, if, as you say, Congress responds more to the media coverage of something happening overseas, how is it that Congress, after a whole summer of Lebanon and front page stories and dominations of evening news, turns around and increases Israel's aid by half a billion dollars against the administration's wishes? If you say Congress is the first to respond to the media, I wonder how you'd explain that.

DAVID NEWSOM: Congress does not respond only to the media. I think there are other pressures as well. But what I really had in mind -- it may be a terrible admission for someone from the State Department -- is that I can't remember a time in which someone said in a policy meeting, "You know, Joe Kraft has got a good idea in his column this morning; we ought to examine it." The question usually is, "How are we going to answer what Joe Kraft said in his column this morning?" But a Congressman will take that column and call up the Secretary and say, "You should look into this." And because it comes from the Congress rather than the newspaper it will get some attention -- not always, but more than it would just by the fact that it is printed in a column. Also, we know from long experience that if a hearing is held, you can prepare to be a witness at a hearing by reading all the briefing books, but the best way to prepare is to read the New York Times and the Washington Post that morning because the chances are that those will be the sources from which the Congressman's questions will come. In that sense, the press reports are a sort of immediate trigger to a reaction by Congress to events, to a greater extent than is true of the Executive branch.

DAVID LICHTENSTEIN: I was struck by your term "deliberate bias." I think it is very difficult to prove that any reporter covering El Salvador or Vietnam was deliberately biased. In the end, the connotation of that phrase is something sinister. Actually, you can get very drastic, unfortunate consequences which are not the result of deliberate bias but a bias that results from a certain perception of social factors that are involved, a lack of historical perspective in covering something like the Lebanon invasion. You might find it very difficult to prove that some of the reporters have distorted reality in covering the Israeli invasion into Lebanon and in showing a deliberate bias toward the PLO. But they did have a certain view of Middle Eastern politics, a very shallow and superficial view of the basic causes which motivated Israel to invade Lebanon. Their perception was guided only by what they saw and wanted to see. The word "deliberate" seems miscast there. You can get a bias but it may not be deliberate. It is a result of the person's ideological preconception.

DAVID NEWSOM: I used the word "purposeful bias."

CARL MIGDAIL: You can also get a purposeful bias and let me define. If you have a sense of historical analysis, a conviction in your mind as to the way the flow of history should go, then a correspondent in the

field can fall into the error of choosing sides.
Choosing the good guys versus the bad guys can shape
his or her reporting. That certainly does happen and
that is not, in the viewpoint of the correspondent,
deceitful. I think in terms of our form of journalism
it is deceitful, but having said that, let me go on to
something else.

I think it is a given in our form of society that
the press -- to use that term as a catchall for all
media coverage -- plays a role in influencing the
policy of the United States government, in its foreign
policy toward the world. It's the way our government
was set up in terms of diverse influences and it is a
reciprocal sort of thing. For example, the
anti-Sandinista guerillas invited two correspondents to
join them in the field in Nicaragua. Now, not only did
they want coverage, but they wanted it for a certain
purpose. And one can deduce that the reason they
wanted it was to prevent the United States government
from pulling back. Since they were unsure about the
extent of continued support by the Reagan
administration, they were bringing the question of
covert operations out into the open.

DAVID LICHTENSTEIN: I would like to suggest that one of
the great problems of contemporary journalism is a
problem of rushing prematurely to the moral judgments
of history. Journalists have become tribunes of the
people. Reporters who were assigned to the Lebanon
incursion, or to Vietnam, or to El Salvador, engage in
instantaneous moral condemnation depending upon their
predilections, their philosophies. Never before in
history have reporters been charged with the enormous
responsibility of engaging in instantaneous moral
condemnation. I'm struck by this because of the fact
that so much of the criticism of the press arises from
this sort of...pro-Arab or pro-Israel bias --
sentiments in favor of Ho Chi Minh or in favor of the
Communist guerillas. You have within the media
ideological conflicts which run all the way across the
political spectrum.

Now compare a journalist with an historian. An
historian, before he engages in moral condemnation,
waits ten or fifteen or twenty years to assemble all
the evidence. It is one of the most baffling problems
for a professional historian who looks at the same sort
of thing that a journalist does; he reviews the
evidence and, to some extent, affixes moral blame where
it is, or lack of moral blame where it is not. But the
historian has the advantage of writing history a
considerable amount of time after the events have
occurred. Needless to say, the journalist who has been
assigned to a war-battle area is trying to catch events

on the fly. And his judgment consequently is a snap moral judgment, not predicated upon a sound appraisal of responsibility, not based upon a sound historical evaluation of all the forces that are at work. He just sees a village being destroyed and he says, "Well, the Israeli guns shattered that village." This is the perspective from which he operates. This is what he sees. He sees this vast range of artillery moving in to a certain coastal town and he's not going to get the whole picture in perspective. He is not an historian; he cannot evaluate all the facts which are involved and which motivated the Israeli government to move into Lebanon.

Essentially, this is true in El Salvador. The whole uproar over human rights, for example, is often the shrill cry of the not-very-well-informed journalistic visitor who lacks historical perspective, who is not familiar with Latin American culture, or how an entirely different culture developed out of entirely different social conditions.

WALTER FRIEDENBERG: I disagree. Take the Vietnam War, for example. It wasn't moral indignation and condemnation that made the American press, by and large, see the war in a certain way. Newspaper people -- I don't care what anybody else will say -- are pragmatic. We are so damn pragmatic, many of us caring only when our next dinner is going to be, that I don't think we are prone to moral indignation or condemnation. Is it going to work? That is the question we ask, again and again. You didn't have to have eyeglasses in the early days of Vietnam to determine that things were not going to work unless other matters were tended to. I disagree.

DAVID LICHTENSTEIN: Are you suggesting that journalists don't engage in moral condemnation?

WALTER FRIEDENBERG: I say we don't. I think we are very pragmatic. We ask ourselves, "Is this policy going to work or not?" and that's our basic concern.

NICK THIMMESCH: I would like to address two of the points Mr. Lichtenstein made. One is that he said the American press made immediate moral judgments, condemnations of U.S. actions in Vietnam. The veteran reporters there in the early years of Vietnam were about as straight as they could be. Charlie Moore and Keys Beech and others were very straight. It was only late in the war, I'd say, that reporting did show a lot of the failures and incongruities and inconsistencies.

Secondly, you said that historians had fifteen years in which they can make their moral condemnation.

I would suggest that from the outset, historians were condemning what Hitler was doing, probably as quickly as our correspondents were doing in Vietnam. I don't think historians waited until 1960 to decide that Hitler was an evil force in the twentieth century. I think the historians were on top of that pretty fast.

DAVID LICHTENSTEIN: You are quite right about that. There is no problem of moral condemnation for the bombing of Dresden, Munich and so on, and yet the slightest infraction by an administration fighting communist-led guerillas leads to immediate condemnation.

PHILIP GEYELIN: A point that I would like to make is that the media is subject to judgments you would never make about any other profession. Of course, coverage is not completely balanced. Access is vital. We're not covering Cambodia. We're not covering Afghanistan. Talking about the early coverage of Vietnam, those reporters really reported the facts as they observed them. I do not find moral condemnation and bias in the coverage of the Lebanon war. The Israelis are accustomed to controlling the game too much. Skepticism is born in the early stages of a situation like wars and conflict. Things don't work out well, and people start asking a lot of difficult questions. That may sound like a moral judgment, but I don't read a moral judgment in television footage or writing about the destruction of a village. It happened, it's a fact. Pretty good coverage was provided of the various atrocities that have been committed inside Israel by Palestinian terrorists in past years. What you can see is what you can write about. West Beirut, the destruction of hospitals and homes, you could see that. You could not see dead PLO guerillas. You were under escort, and that does slant coverage.

Back to the Third World -- large parts of it are inaccessible. Since we are in a visual age, what you can't see, can't hurt you. I find this question of moral pronouncements a misreading of the ways reporters think and write.

DAVID NEWSOM: If I can move back to the question of the day, my impression from having been in the government is that, with perhaps the exception of a few conversations that may take place between a very prominent and respected reporter or editor and high government officials, the relationship of the reporters in Washington to officials is basically a relationship of questions and answers. It is not a relationship based on an exchange of views. If this is so, it is somewhat regrettable and merits more examination

because in many ways the correspondents who have
covered the State Department and the White House have
been there through several administrations. They
outlast almost all of the key officials in any State
Department. Their long-term knowledge of events and
personalities is probably greater than that of many of
the officials they are dealing with. And yet, I have
very little impression of an exchange beyond questions
and answers. There is very seldom a sharing of
assessments. Is this a correct impression as seen from
the press side or not?

DAVID LICHTENSTEIN: A quick summary of the ideological
conflict is contained in some of the printed materials
distributed to us. One statement says: "U.S. media has
a consistent liberal bias in favor of Latin American
revolutionaries." Another says: "U.S. media has served
American interests well and has shown poverty and
oppression and Latin American corruption...." Here you
have completely divergent perceptions of what are the
basic economic and social problems of Latin America.
    Now, a reporter who believes the thesis of the
second quote, that the Sandinistas or the communist
guerillas really represent the true aspirations of the
peasants of Latin America and that the basic forces for
revolutionary activity in Latin America are poverty and
depression, has a certain perception which guides or
controls his reporting. The mindset of the reporter
controls what he or she perceives. You have two points
of view which are so diametrically in conflict that
they cannot be reconciled. It affects public opinion
which, in turn, causes the President to worry. He
looks over his shoulder constantly at what the
Washington Post is saying. He looks at the fact that
he's got a thousand reporters on the Honduras border
saying, "My God, the United States is engaging in
covert operations." It seems we can no more engage in
covert operations than fish in a fishbowl. That has an
enormous impact on what the President does.

PHILIP GEYELIN: Well, you have something a bit more
solid to go on than a reporter's presumed biases. You
have a recent independent commission report, prepared
by forty-six people, half of them Latin Americans and
half of them North Americans -- some of those Americans
included David Rockefeller, Frank Shakespeare, David
Jones, the former head of the Joint Chiefs -- and if
there was one point on which they were unanimous, it
was that economic poverty, with one-third of the people
in abject poverty, is the underlying cause of the
problem. That is not based on some liberal reporter's
perceptions.

MARK FALCOFF: It strikes me that neither of these perceptions is totally true or totally false. Both have some policy-specific implications. And both the Carter and Reagan administrations, in different policy-specific ways, reflect both of these viewpoints. It was, after all, the Carter administration which cut off aid to the Sandinistas. It was the Carter administration that decided to resume arms shipments to El Salvador.

I have been unhappy with media coverage of Central America, but I must say that I don't think the media can be faulted for not being any more clear about the issues than the policy makers have been. The center of gravity of policy toward Central America has shifted back and forth for the last three or four years. I think some of the complaints that have been made about the media are nothing more than a reflection of this fact.

CARL MIGDAIL: I have a feeling that there is a great lack of realism here; that is, lack of factual realism. There is a covert action going on against Nicaragua. I was in the region a year ago and found it then. The only question is will it continue and will it be successful? It is covert in that it has never been publicly revealed by the President, even though he has hinted at it for different reasons.

Now, on the question of whether correspondents are unusually skeptical of their own government, I assure you that most correspondents would prefer to back their government as far as possible. When there is skepticism, it is because a rational human being, who is a correspondent, who is a so-called expert in the field, knows that government facts are not facts but lies. Let me give you one example. There isn't the slightest indication from the Soviet Union nor from the Nicaraguan government that Soviet missiles will be emplaced in Nicaragua. I know the derivation of that rumor. Assistant Secretary Tom Enders -- he should not have done it -- picked it up and then the Secretary picked it up.

I'd like to say something about two different kinds of reporting. You can do a report on the bombing of our embassy in Beirut and talk about the horror of the bodies, or you can do an analysis of why it took place in Beirut and who possibly is involved. Then, you are a total fool if you do not know the history of the Middle East. If you do not know the internal, political, and economic movements in each of the countries in the Middle East, you cannot put together a cohesive picture of the dynamic forces at work in Beirut. If you were reporting on Nicaragua in 1978 and 1979, somewhere along the line, if you were a scrupulous correspondent, conscious of your responsibility to the American people, you would have had to point out why there was a national consensus, led by Archbishop Obando y Bravo, to overthrow the regime, and which led conservatives to form a coalition with the Sandinistas. Now, on the other hand, I know of no correspondent either within the United States or Central America, who is reporting today that the Sandinistas are an answer to the economic and social poverties of Nicaragua.

On the question of the reporting of bodies found in El Salvador, I submit to you that eighty-five or ninety percent of all human rights atrocities in El Salvador have been committed by the right. And I can prove it to you; I have been there time and time again. So please, it is not an abstract question. When you come upon a disfigured body, it's a fact, it's a human being and, in the context of where it takes place, it is not difficult to figure out who did it. Does the left kill? Yes. Does the left commit atrocities in El Salvador? Yes, but so does the right and in greater numbers. One should not forget that at all.

PAT ELLIS: I would like to go back to something that was said earlier. I would like to argue that the administration, to a large extent, sets the foreign news agenda.

Take El Salvador. I remember that fateful February day when everyody was gathered in the briefing room of the State Department and we were told that the line was being drawn in El Salvador. It wasn't the reporters that were doing that, it was the administration that was setting the agenda. Periodically, the attention devoted to El Salvador has abated. But time and time again, the administration sets the agenda for the media, despite some bit of investigative reporting, and it's usually just a matter of the reporter following up the agenda the administration has set. There are many other examples.

DANIEL JAMES: I want to come back to the issue of "moral indignation" -- and I really don't think that is the right term. What has come to be known as advocacy journalism must be recognized as a fact of media life today. Reporters go out there and say they are reporting on a situation when, in fact, they are writing editorials or what is sometimes called "news analysis." That is fine as long as the correct label is used, "editorial" or "opinion." This kind of reporting, I submit, is often flawed by a lack of historical knowledge of different situations, whether in the Middle East or in Central America or in some

other region of the world. I have just completed a
study of media coverage of El Salvador over a three
year period, examining some thousands of articles and
op-ed pieces. From all of that I conclude: there has
been a total misperception of Salvadoran history,
history as written by the historians, of which the
media representatives have been largely ignorant. For
example, they talk of the fifty years of repression in
El Salvador which antedated the taking of power by the
young military officers in October 1979, as if there
had been a continuum here of military dictatorship from
1932 to the present. This is absolutely untrue; it's a
complete misreading of that country's history. The
dictatorship to which they are referring was overthrown
in 1944. After that they had a series of interregnums,
during which there was some semblance of democratic
government emerging. As a result of such
misconceptions, however, the media have built up in the
minds of the U.S. public an image of the current
government of El Salvador as the continuation of a
long-ago dictatorship.

A second point. Since shortly after the October
'79 coup in El Salvador, the U.S. media have raised the
cry that we are getting involved in a quagmire, a
"Vietnam quagmire." I believe it was the Washington
Post that started using that phrase back in February of
1980. Now the junta had been in office maybe four or
five months. There were no U.S. military advisors in
El Salvador at the time. Yet, immediately, the spectre
of another Vietnam was raised by the media. At the
same time, there was a movement afoot to oppose any
military aid the United States government may have been
considering but had not yet decided on. I am talking
here of a time and set of circumstances during the
Carter administration. A trend immediately developed
of opposition to military aid. The trend has continued
-- to arouse American public opinion against aid to El
Salvador, even though the aide has been predominantly
economic, whereas military aid is relatively much less
-- and certainly minor compared to the money we are
dishing out to Israel and a lot of other countries.
Why this obsession of the media to raise the scare of
another Vietnam in relation to El Salvador? Why does no
one raise the bogey of Vietnam with regard to Lebanon,
a far more dangerous, far more explosive situtation,
and far more likely to involve the United States in
warfare than anything we can foresee in El Salvador?

PHILIP GEYELIN: First with respect to Lebanon,
everybody from Barry Goldwater to Ted Kennedy has
raised the spectre of Vietnam in connection with our
sending Marines to Lebanon. It started in the Congress
with discussion of the War Powers Resolution. Exactly

those reservations were expressed about our move into Lebanon.

DANIEL JAMES: I will correct myself. There have been some of those comments about Lebanon. But make a comparison between the number of media reports raising the threat of a Vietnam in El Salvador and the number of such items written today about the spectre of a Vietnam in Lebanon, and you will agree that the former have been much louder."

PHILIP GEYELIN: I was talking about the media being carefully read. In addition to reporters going down to El Salvador, there is a steady stream of Congressmen doing down. As a covert operation is being conducted against Nicaragua, we have had five who went down on a CIA plane, which raises some questions about the covertness of it. Those people are getting their views first hand, not through the media.

WALTER FRIEDENBERG: Let me make two points. I agree with David Newsom's mild note about the skepticism of the press. But I don't think that is a conspicuous current trend. It may have been exacerbated by Vietnam and Watergate; but I disagree with Daniel James' notion about our becoming a pack of advocates. We are not that conspiratorial; we're not that sheep-like; we are not given to herdish tendencies. But what we won't do, and we have this constitutional function, is take the word from the White House or the Congress or any other governmental authority as sacred writ. We don't work for Izvestia or Pravda. We have a free press. Historical ignorance? Yes. Naivete? Yes. Personal bias? Yes. Skewed access? I'm sorry, but that's the case. How far is it from the hotel? Will you get shot by going there? But we are not reformers. We are not trying to bend U.S. policy. We are just trying to cover Nicaragua in Nicaragua. And we are trying to cover U.S. policy toward Nicaragua in Washington. Every time the president or someone opens his mouth to tell us not to worry, everything is all right, then it is our constitutional duty to say, "Let's take a look."

PAT ELLIS: I would like to bring up another point on El Salvador. In addition to all the reporters and Congressmen who go down there, you have the representatives of organizations siding with either the left or the right point of view. I am the recipient of all kinds of lobbying on this issue, constantly getting knocks on my door and being given all that literature, so much information on all sides of the issue.

CARL MIGDAIL: I leave the different interpretations of

Salvadoran history, from 1932 to 1979, for private discussion with Dan James. We could probably work that bit of history over for a year.

I agree with Pat Ellis on this question of the reciprocal arrangement of journalists influencing government and government influencing us. On March 28, 1982, there were 800 correspondents of all kinds in Salvador. They thought the country would explode. And remembering back a short time earlier when another correspondent and I were the only two foreign correspondents in the country, I can assure you that despite any change that had taken place in that country, it had not increased 800-fold or 400-fold in importance or quality of newsworthiness. All of the correspondents in the world, or their editors, were simply reacting to Secretary Al Haig's statement that in El Salvador "the future of the free world" was being resolved. So, we respond in terms of our coverage in exactly the way our government and other major governments define the issues.

Then on the question of whether we have access, that is one of the myths that patronizes. We are told, "If you knew better, if you were brighter, more educated, had better access -- then you would not make the stupid mistakes you do." This attitude is very condescending. I do not know of any responsible correspondent who is ultimately defeated by lack of access. We are not a uniform group. We are the most diverse collection of different personalities in any profession you can think of. We rarely share information with each other and we are individualistic in coming to our conclusions. Many of us have excellent access in countries where we work: to presidents, cabinet ministers, leaders in the opposition, to all kinds of people who should be heard. If we make errors, it is not because of lack of access.